THE   GREEN   WIC

Twelve gates there are in Heaven's wall,
Round the city clear as glass,
And every gate is made of pearl
Through which the pure souls pass.

Apostles stand at the gates of pearl,
But by this wicket green,
He who doth save both man and beast,
The Lord Himself is seen.

He calls his creatures to come in,
And opens the wicket wide,
And the poor things, when they hear His voice,
Flock through to the other side.

Tired horses and mangy cats,
And poor lost dogs are there,
And little birds once cramped and caged,
Come singing through the air.

Fair is the city of golden streets,
With the gates of pearl flung wide,
Let us come to the Wicket Green,
And stand by the Master's side.

(Dog Sanctuary Poem)

In a time when the Earth was veiled in mystery many thousand years ago, relative peace and harmony reigned, as humans sought to live in accord with the energies of Nature. It preceded the patriarchal order with its emphasis on laws, social ideals and political aims, in marked contrast to the worship of the Great Mother from whose sacred womb, emerges every living thing.

The glory and wonder of Mother Nature, universally revered, was given expression by imbuing everything with divinity. The Great Goddess was portrayed in archetypal, symbolic terms which modern savants are able to interpret through the study of context and association.

In her important work 'The Language of the Goddess', the eminent Archaeologist, Marija Gimbutas tells us: 'The world of the Goddess implies the whole realm in which she manifested herself. Her place in prehistory and in early history as a cosmogenic figure, the universal fruitful Source, is no longer a novelty to many readers...she has been described as the Great Mother who gives birth to all things from her womb...figurines found in quantity in almost every Neolithic settlement and cemetery are invaluable for reconstructing not only the symbolism but the religion itself...the main theme of Goddess symbolism is the mystery of birth and death and the renewal of life, not only human but all life on earth and indeed in the whole cosmos. Symbols and images cluster around the parthenogenetic (self-generating) Goddess and her basic functions as Giver of Life, Wielder of Death, and, not less importantly, as Regeneratrix, and around the Earth Mother, the Fertility Goddess young and old, rising and dying with plant life...this symbolic system represents cyclical, not linear, mythical time.'

The Ancient Egyptians worshipped the Great Mother in her many aspects. One of them, Bastet the Cat Goddess, was venerated, in her sacred Temple at Bubaste, where she represented her benign aspect as opposed to the redoubtable Sekmet, her sister. The cat possesses both lunar and solar aspects,

In the Hadith which contain the Sayings of the Prophet Muhammad, there are these teachings: "Whoever is kind to a beast is as good as doing good to a human being.'while an act of cruelty to a beast is as bad as an act of cruelty to a human being.'

Dostoevsky, the great writer, wrote some wise words in his 'Brothers Karamasov': 'Divine Love is the highest love on earth. Love all God's creation, the whole and every grain of sand in it. Love every leaf, every ray of God's light. Love the animals, love the plants, love everything. If you love everything, you will perceive the divine mystery in things. Once you perceive it, you will begin to comprehend it better every day. And you will come at last to love the whole world with an all-embracing love. Love the animals: God has given them the rudiments of thought and joy untroubled. Do not trouble it, don't harass them, don't deprive them of their happiness, don't work against God's intent. Man, do not pride yourself on superiority to the animals; they are without sin, and you, with your greatness, defile the earth by your appearance on it, and leave the traces of your foulness after you – alas, it is true of almost every one of us!.....always decide to use humble love. If you resolve on that once for all, you may subdue the whole world......Brothers, love is a teacher; but one must know how to acquire it, for it is hard to acquire, it is dearly bought, it is won slowly by long labour. For we must love not only occasionally, for a moment, but for ever. ...My brother asked the birds to forgive him; that sounds senseless, but it is right; for all is like an ocean, all is flowing and blending; a touch in one place sets up movement at the other end of the earth. It may be senseless to beg forgiveness of the birds, but birds would be happier at your side – a little happier, anyway – and children, and all animals, if you were nobler than you are now. It's all like an ocean, I tell you. Then you would pray to the birds too, consumed by an all-embracing love, in a sort of transport, and pray that they too will forgive you your sin. Treasure this ecstasy, however senseless it may seem to men.'

*   *   *

There are countless tales about holy men and women who exemplified this close communing with the Sacred in their own lives.

One such, was an old Arab traveller whose caravan stopped for the night. Upon scooping out the sugar for this tea, he discovered some ants in it.

'Ah,' thought he, 'I have taken them far from their relatives, for they were not there when I last opened this tin.'

Without further ado, he ordered the caravan to turn back until they reached their last halting site. Very gently, the holy man laid the contents of his tin on the golden desert sands. 'There, little ones,' he said to the ants, 'go back to your families, as I return to mine.'

A Christian monk once toiled in the field near his hermitage. As he was hot, he lay his cloak on the ground near some bushes.

When his work was done, he went to the spot to pick up his cloak, whereupon he discovered that a sparrow had laid her eggs on it and was brooding them.

He smiled at her: 'Little mother-to-be, remain where you are. I shall not disturb you.'

With that, he went to his small hut where his strange pets awaited him. The cock perched on his bed where the holy man slept, crowing loudly when it was time for Matins. A tame cricket played its musical legs as the hermit sang the praises of the Holy One, and later, a tame fly kept the hermit's rhythm when reading, by hopping from word to word, as though performing a service for the monk.

The cloak remained where it was until the Sparrow family departed of their own accord.

Saint Rose of Lima was once asked by a priest who visited her small room in her parents' garden, why it was that he was so tormented by mosquitoes on a summer's evening, while she was left alone.

Giving him one of her lovely smiles, she replied: 'We have an understanding. I do not pester them, and they in turn do not bother me.'

This answer did not entirely convince the priest however, who watched with amazement as a cloud of mosquitoes bunched together above the fair maiden's head as she began to pray. They appeared to be 'buzzing', as though intoning their own hymns of praise!

Saint Francis of Assisi beheld the Sacred in all God's creation. One day he came upon a young man who was going to sell some wild doves he had caught. The Saint, moved by compassion, regarded the gentle animals with pity. 'Young man,' he said, 'I entreat you to give me these harmless creatures, so that they do not fall into cruel hands which would surely put them to death.' The youth acceded to this request, whereupon Saint Francis took them to his bosom, addressing them thus: 'O my little sister, the doves, so simple, so innocent, and so pure, why did you allow yourselves to be caught? I will keep you from a cruel death and make nesting places for you…' Then Saint Francis made nests for the doves where they settled peacefully.

Upon another occasion the Saint came to the city of Gubbio where a large wolf terrorized the inhabitants who went about their daily duties armed, and in great fear of their lives. Feeling pity for the stricken populace, Saint Francis decided to pay a visit to this fierce animal.

He had perforce to go alone, as no one had the temerity to accompany him, following only at a safe distance. When the wolf espied the man, he sprang towards him. Undaunted, Saint Francis made the sign of the Cross, then called out: 'Come here, brother Wolf. I order you, in the name of Christ, to do me no harm, neither to anybody else.'

The wolf lay down at the holy man's feet, meek and submissive, listening to the words addressed to him: 'Brother Wolf, you have done much evil in this land…all men cry out against you…and the city's inhabitants are your enemies, but I will make peace between you and them, O brother Wolf…offend them no longer, and they will forgive you for what you have done. Do you agree?'

For answer, the great wolf bowed his head, signalling with eyes and tail his assent. When Saint Francis had asked him three times if he consented to pledge himself to peace, the Saint took the wolf's paw in his hand, thus sealing the pact. From that day on, the wolf caused no more trouble, fed by the city's inhabitants till he ended his days there. When the wolf died, the townspeople had his body placed in their Church.

Saint Anthony of Padua came one morning to the town of Rimini, where he preached for several days. The citizens paid him little heed however, seeing which he placed himself on a bank between the river and the sea, addressing himself to the fishes: 'Listen to the word of God, O ye fishes of the sea and of the river, seeing that the faithless refuse to do so.' No sooner had the Saint uttered these words than a great multitude of fishes gathered, ranging themselves in perfect order and most peacefully, keeping their heads out of the water, seemingly attentive to the Saint's words: 'My brothers and sisters the fishes, you are bound, as much as is in your power, to give thanks to your Creator, who has given you so noble an element to reside in; for you may choose between sweet and salt water; you have places of refuge from the storm; also, you have a pure and clear element for your nourishment...because of these and many other blessings conferred on you, you are bound to praise and bless the Lord.'

When the holy man finished his talk, the fishes opened their mouths, bowed their heads, seeking in this manner to express their reverence; seeing which Saint Anthony said: 'Blessed be the eternal God, for the fishes of the sea pay homage to Him more than do men of no faith.'

Witnessing the astonishing spectacle of the devout fishes, the people marvelled, and grace touched their hearts, enabling them to receive the spiritual fruit so generously offered them by the Saint.

Sri Ramana Maharshi, the Sage of Arunachala in South India, treated all creatures with a great and tender regard.

A cow called Lakshmi could not keep away from the Sage. She left her stall to climb the hill, seeking out this very special person. Eventually, her owner asked the Sage to adopt her, which he did, and until her death, Lakshmi was devoted to the Sage, Every day, at the same hour, she would take up a position at the door of the Meditation Hall, waiting for the Maharshi. He would emerge, put an arm about her neck, and they would stroll off together. When she was dying, Sri Ramana Maharshi placed one hand on her heart, the other on her forehead, remaining thus, until her glowing, loving eyes closed. The Sage presided over her burial.

To the hermitage of this Sage of modern times, came troops of monkeys, emerging from the nearby groves of trees. They would bring their grievances to the Sage, who listened patiently to what they chattered so excitedly about, then, a quiet would settle over the group as peace reigned.

Nimble monkey fingers would reach for the nuts which the Sage would then distribute amongst them.

One day, a monkey was found lying hurt near the Ashram. He was cared for, named Nondi the Lame. It was his privilege to sit on the Sage's lap at meal-times.

A bird tried several times to build her nest close to the Sage. Each time, an attendant knocked it down, until the Sage said: 'Little mother, how hard you struggle to build your home. Well, we shall see.'

At once the culprit realized he must not refuse the bird. Another spot was chosen in the Hall for the nest to be built, and so the triumphant mother-bird hatched her eggs near the Love-presence of the Sage. They remained there for quite some time.

When pups were born in the Ashram grounds, the Sage had the mother and her babies placed in a comfortable basket, and had her forehead painted with tumeric as a sign of honour paid to her motherhood.

Whenever the Sage went on his daily walk around the holy Mountain, Arunachala, many people observed a strange phenomenon described by the authors of 'The Secret Life of Plants'.

"In South India, McInness witnessed the strange spectacle of Ramana Mohan Maharshi on his evening walk. Within seconds of his leaving the house, cattle tied up in stalls in the village half a mile away would struggle to get out of their ties. When released they careered along the road to accompany the old man on his walk, followed by all the dogs and children of the village. Before the procession had gone very far wild animals and even snakes joined in from the jungle. Thousands of birds appeared, almost blotting out the sky. There were tiny tits, huge kites, heavy-winged vultures and other birds of prey, all flying in harmony around the Maharshi on his walk. When he returned to his room, said McInnes, all the birds, animals and children would quietly disappear.' 1

Once, two scorpions climbed over the Sage's body. The Master remained very calm, unmoving. Presently the scorpions moved away, to the relief of those watching. The Sage reassured them: 'They crawl over you just as they would crawl on the floor or the wall or a tree. Do they crawl over these stinging as they go? It is only because you fear them and do something, that they fear you and do something in return.'

Sri V. Shastri continues with his reminiscences: 'There were two peacocks which used to strut with their feathers spread out like a spangled fan. A cobra too used to take part in this pastime and raised its hood and moved about in their midst.'

Another devotee recollects: 'In the Skandashram days (where the first hermitage was located), the good fortune of taking food with Bhagavan was equally available to birds, animals, and human devotees. Bhagavan never distinguished between his human and animal devotees; the same compassion was available to all.'

A delightful portrait is handed down to us by Sri Narayana: '...in the kitchen garden near the veranda – we saw a small goat, a little monkey, a squirrel – and Sri Bhagavan Ramana Maharshi. Bhagavan was sitting on his haunches with his legs folded up to his breast. The goat nestled between his knees; the monkey had its head resting on his right knee; the squirrel was perched on his left knee. Holding a packet of paper in his left palm, Bhagavan picked up groundnuts from it with his right hand fingers, one by one, and fed the goat, the monkey, the squirrel, and himself, by turns... all the four seemed to be equally happy. They way they looked at one another and kept close together was touching.'

Even trees were not excluded from Bhagavan's love; 'You may call a tree a standing man, and a man a walking tree,' the Sage said. 2

What peace, what joy, reigned in the presence of the Maharshi!
Peacocks danced before him, a golden mongoose seated itself on his lap, squirrels rested on their bushy tails, the dogs lay quietly nearby, children played!

The divine harmony of Love!

*   *   *

TREAD LIGHTLY LITTLE FEET
* * * * * * * * * * * * * * * *

Tread lightly little feet,
And harm not the small ones
Who wander helpless
On the ground.

Busy ants, industrious and tiny,
Place their lives in your care.
Tread lightly, little feet.

The cricket gaily rubbing
His musical, dainty legs
Sings on unaware
Of the danger near him.
Tread lightly, little feet.

A grasshopper takes a rest
On the bright, green lawn.
The golden sun warms him.
Tread lightly, little feet.

Gorgeously- coloured butterfly
Spreads its wings and
Lies directly in your path.
Tread lightly, little feet.

For kill not intentionally
The small, trusting creatures.
Rather, marvel at their wonder,
And let them live,
By treading lightly, little feet.

-The Author

THE WAY

_____

Mauritius is a beautiful Jewel-island reposing like a pearl in the turquoise oyster of the Indian Ocean.

It is there that my grandmother Maya, and her younger sister, Antoinette, decided to help a sick cat who, in their opinion, was mortally ill.

There were no veterinary clinics on the island in those days, so that animals received no professional care when they were ill or hurt.

Maya had talked her sister into helping her this summer day.

They had managed to procure some Ether and cottonwool.

The sick cat lay on the table, eyes closed.

Maya held the bottle of ether, her sister had a wad of cottonwool stretched out in both palms.

'Now, hold very still,' Maya said, 'I am going to pour the ether on to the cottonwool. Then, we will place it over our cat's nose.'

Very carefully, the twelve-year-old bent to her task.

Suddenly, there was a yowl, a ball of fur bounded through the open window, whilst two young girls fell to the floor, having placed their noses too close to the ether-soaked cotton-wool.

Undaunted by their first failure at playing Vets, when they were grown up, my grandmother and her sister succeeded in forming a circle of animal Carers on the Island.

It was to this maternal grandmother I came, when I was eight years old, carrying a sick cat in my arms, tears running down my cheeks, heart heavy with sadness.

'Ma petite, don't cry,' were her words, as she ushered me into the room, 'don't cry. Here, give me the cat. Sit down, wipe your eyes.'

'Grandmother, her poor eyes are sick,' I sobbed, pointing to the inflamed orbs in question.

'I can see that,' my grandmother replied, 'but it is not as serious as it looks. I have something that will help at once.'

In no time at all the cat was made comfortable, an ointment had been introduced into her sick eyes, and a small pink tongue was busily tasting some fresh milk which held liberal dollops of cream.

My grandmother drew me to her side.

She was petite, with a very beautiful face which was dominated by eyes of rare beauty both in size and colour, being of an emerald green.

Her glance was gentle, so was her voice: 'My little one, from this day, your sensitive heart will walk its own path. But, remember this. You cannot help ALL who suffer. We have, each and every one of us, a beginning called birth, and an end called death. We walk, from the day we are born, to the day we die, a certain distance, if you like. It is like a race clearly marked out for a runner. Whatever is placed on this track or road, must be attended to, with all the compassion we have. As I said, you will not be able to help everyone or every thing, but whatever is placed in your path, whether it be a rock, plant, an animal, an insect, or a human being – you must do your very best for them. Above all, treat all with HEART. Then, when the time comes to leave this world, your heart will be calm and peaceful – you will have tried...'

'But Grandmother, what if I don't always remember this?'

The green eyes smiled at me: 'Ah, we all forget...but when that happens, do not beat your poor heart with harsh remorse – just get up, shake yourself, and try again. One does not learn this great lesson in a day or a year – it takes a lifetime, and even then, many of us have still not walked the Road in a Sacred manner. We can but try – very hard.'

She hugged me, enclosing me with her dainty, but strong arms: 'Just do your best. Love – love – love! As you did today! Do not worry about this cat-person. I will look after her.'

After that, I brought the starving and sick cats I found, to Grandmother Maya. She would use, among other things, a strong-smelling 'Blue' soap, Condy's crystals (Potassium Permanganate), and Herbal remedies. Invariably, she cured them.

My parents began calling me their 'phenomenon', but I was too young to understand what that long word meant.

Grandmother Maya had lost her husband when she was twenty-eight years of age. She had loved him so deeply, that years later, when asked why she refused to remarry, she replied: 'My heart is a plant whose roots are in Heaven.'

She had withdrawn from the world after her husband's death, had become a Franciscan Tertiary, which had so alarmed her son and two daughters, that they had secretly done away with her brown robes.

When the grieving widow spent her days tending sick animals, and nursing the poor of Mauritius in their hovels, her family were horrified. They exerted pressure on her to desist visiting lepers, and cases of Tuberculosis, whereupon the headstrong Maya took her children, and sailed off for Madagascar, where she became the Editor of a Newspaper in Tamatave, as well as being a Music Teacher. She was an accomplished pianist. The sick and abandoned animals of Tamatave received her care and attention.

Somehow, this Trail 'which led from Grandmother to grandchild, a kind of 'animal magic' began to unfold in my life.

My parents always fostered cats and dogs, so that we grew up with pets gracing our household.

When Grandmother Maya came to live with us, she brought her pets with her.

The years passed, flowing by like a swift river of starlight.

One day Grandmother Maya called me to her side: 'I have a great favour to ask of you. As you know, Bijou died yesterday. The Vet has taken her away, and he has promised me that he would perform an autopsy on her.'

Her voice dropped to a whisper: 'I know the other members of the family might think I am being foolish or becoming senile, if I ask them to check Bijou's body for me. As you know, I usually keep the body of my dead pets for three days before burial, but in this case, the Vet has taken her away, and I am sorry to have to say this, but I cannot put my faith in anyone as far as animal welfare is concerned.' She paused, 'You will understand. Many people think it is sentimental and silly to love animals as intensely as we do. Yet, this is because it is they who have lost their way – not we, ours! One can call oneself religious, and yet not be religious at all! An animal is the visible expression of the Divine Glory…it is not silly nor sentimental to truly love these creatures of God. I hear people say that animals have no souls, and this horrifies me! How can one say one believes in an Omnipresent God, if in the next breath one declares Divine Creation lacks soul? Is one saying then 'Yes, I believe in God – but this God is limited to dwelling in Man? 'To believe such a thing is nonsense! So, will you do this for me, my little one?'

'Of course, Grandmother. I will call your Vet and tell him I am coming.'

That afternoon I drove over to Sandown Veterinary Clinic, just outside Johannesburg, where I was presented with a jute bag by a helper who had a puzzled look on her face.

I took it from her and walked outside to where the Jacaranda trees were ablaze with purple blooms, leafy branches sparkling in the clear light.

Placing the sack on the fragrant grass, I scrutinised the contents. When I was satisfied that it contained the remains of Bijou (Jewel), I said a prayer, returned the bag to the Assistant, and told my Grandmother that she need have no fear that Bijou would be interred whilst still alive.

Two years later, I rushed a beautiful Ridgeback to the Clinic, with Grandmother seated ashen-faced beside me, as I directed the car speedily round the bends of the road. We were too late to save her pet. We watched as the Vet placed a bar in the dog's jaws, as efforts were made to pump the canine's stomach of the strychnine poison which had been placed in his food by some cruel stranger.

I was as pale as my Grandmother as we watched the Ridgeback agonise, and finally, expire.

Some dark hearts perform dark deeds.

*   *   *

MIKO

Grandmère Maya's sister, Aunt Ines, came from Mauritius to live in Johannesburg, in South Africa.

One day, her husband daughter, and son-in-law were killed when the car in which they travelled was involved in a collision on the Petersburg Road near Johannesburg.

I brought my aunt to our home, where she stayed for six months.

With her, came a Manx cat called Miko which had been the pet of Tante Ines's husband.

Miko was coal-black, with large, golden eyes. His personality was an amiable one, but, having been exclusively my uncle Joseph's favourite, he kept himself rather aloof from other people as a consequence.

Tante Ines kept a close watch over Miko, knowing how deeply attached her husband had been to him.

My son Guillaume, a teenager at the time, decided to play a prank on her. Accordingly, he crept into my mother's room, found a black wig she had just procured for herself from a wandering salesman, and pushed it through Tante Ines's bedroom window.

The old lady bent down.

'Miko, my darling Miko!'

No movement. Stillness.

'Miko! Miko! Miko!'

Next, a piercing shriek, my name being called.

'What is it, Tante Ines?'

Eyes awash with tears, trembling fingers indicating the inert black fur, my aunt whispered: 'Something terrible has happened. Miko fell through the window. He is not moving. He must be dead. Someone has murdered him!'

In a trice I had picked up the glossy fur.

'It is all right, Tante Ines. It is only a wig. Look!'

By this time, muffled giggles coming from under the window suddenly ceased. A disconcerted face peered into the room: 'It was only a joke, Tante. I am sorry you got so upset.'

The matriarch rounded on my son. I listened as the teenager received a choice of such ladylike but strong language as would have scorched the very fires of a volcano...

Having delivered her: 'You must show respect for your elders...our white hairs are not to be denigrated ...in the old days such disrespect would have been severely dealt with, young man. There was chivalry, honour...'

And now, a twinkle and a lovely smile: 'I forgive you this time, but no next time. Is that clear? Go and play your games on someone of your own level of intelligence. You may fetch me my medicine from the bathroom shelf. I have all my system in disorder due to this sudden raid on my emotions.'

She sailed towards her wardrobe, took out the key tied to the thread about her throat, carefully plaited to looked like a necklace, inserted the key into the keyhole, and reached for her bottle of Cinzano Vermouth. Drawing out her small glass kept there for medicinal purposes, Tante Ines poured herself a 'tot' which she downed in one gulp.

'There! That will steady me for the night.'

I watched this ritual every day, fascinated.

Taking a blue pencil from her drawer, my aunt placed the 'marker' on the level of her Cinzano. In this way, when was able to see at a glance whether anyone had 'tampered' with her 'medicine'.

When my aunt left our home, Miko went with her.

Four days later he was back. I opened the kitchen door to see what indeed looked like a limp wig. Gently, I picked it up.

One golden eye peered at me, the other was hidden by the flow of crimson pouring from an awful wound near the left ear.

I cried out, lifted Miko, carried him into the living room, where I located a cushion on which I lowered him gently, feeling his soft breath on my cheek as I did so. Miko made no sound. He was totally exhausted, his fur matted with dried blood and dirt.

A frantic phone-call to the Vet, then back again to Miko's side, where the golden eye continued to regard me with unwavering and loving gaze.

I wept. 'Miko, you came back. You found your way to me.'

How had he done it?

I had driven him and my aunt some distance in my car, from Observatory to Hillbrow, a distance of about six miles, yet he had managed to walk all the way back to our home!

My friend, Mr Davis our vet, was by my side in no time at all. After a quick check, he told me: 'I will take him back with me right away. He has been fighting a very strong Tom, and he is in bad shape. Still, I will do all I can to pull him through. First thing though, this injection to take away the pain.'

With practised skill, Doctor Davis attended to the cat, then Miko was whisked away to the Surgery.

Meanwhile, my aunt Ines, in tears, had sent her maid out in one direction whilst she searched in another, for the cat her late husband had so loved.

When I informed her that Miko had arrived on my doorstep, she could scarce believe her ears.

Some hours later, I was at the animal Clinic, looking at the inert figure of brave Miko, the daring adventurer - explorer extraordinaire – the bold hero, who dared to cross streets filled with car-wizards under whose wheels a cat-person was sure to dice with death. He had braved the unknown. Step by step, he had sniffed the air, taking in the petrol fumes, the pollen drifting like fine cobwebs in the sunlight...as I drove Miko home, I visualized him padding hour after hour on the warm pavements, taking in the noise of heavy traffic, human sounds and smells, scenting danger as the thug Tom-cat sprang out at him. Then, I could imagine the scene, as the terrible fight for survival was played out somewhere, Miko striking out with claws slashing, and teeth tearing and biting. He had been severely wounded. The doctor had had to remove the damaged eye, but thankfully, Miko was still alive.

My Aunt Ines had told me that I could keep Miko. She said he had earned the right to choose where he wished to live. I had been grateful to her for her kindness, as I too, was of the opinion that Miko had undertaken a long and courageous journey, had sacrificed an eye, to be with us. The least I could do was welcome him into our home. He had already made himself at home in my heart!

A few more weeks, and Miko was in splendid form. His fur became glossy once more, he put on weight and muscle, walking with unhurried, majestic pace around the property, his one amber eye glowing with happiness.

I observed him as he created a routine for himself the way cat-persons do. A delicate flick of the tail, a sharp, quick look round, a sniff at the cushion, the head cocked a little to one side like inquisitive bird, a long look at me whilst he gauged whether I was settling for a time or still gadding about, then, a leisurely stretch before assuming a comfortable position.

We both observed each other, grew to know what special 'looks' meant; the silent language of the heart.

Miko had been with us several months when the cat-person he was to love very much entered our lives.

NOU-NOU

It was love at first sight for me.

I saw her from across the busy city street, a small black bundle leaning against the warmth of the building which was Harrison Street Car Park.

I came to her side even as her dainty paw passed ever so gently across the cut on her nose. She was dirty, painfully thin, obviously ill, as she trembled from weakness and no doubt, from hunger.

Yet, she stopped her attempts at a toilette to look at me with big eyes in which there was no trace of self-pity. My heart gave a leap. Tears misted my sight.

I scooped her into my arms, held her cupped in the hollow of my throat as I made my way swiftly to my car.

She made no move. Instead, her skeletal frame rested quietly against me, trusting this human-person instinctively.

Her courage shone like the midday sun.

There was no reasoning process necessary here. My heart knew that this Cat-lady possessed a rare, unique spirit. She had suffered, somehow had managed to survived in this concrete jungle, and, although I could never hope to explain my inner machinations to anyone, within my deep self I knew I had always known and loved her.

These first movements of my heart proved to be true, for later, throughout the many years we spent together, Nou-Nou's sterling qualities never dimmed but only grew brighter.

It was only when the car moved, that Nou-Nou, for her name had crystallised immediately in my mind, began to be restless. I quietened her with soothing words until once home, I took her again in my arms, this time to carry her inside.

I placed her in a comfortable place in the dining-room, prepared some food, a water dish, then, a milk-saucer, which I placed near to her. She drank only water.

Once again, my friend the Vet, promised to come as soon as he could.

Miko, meanwhile, was behaving strangely.

His majestic, languid air had deserted him. Instead, he huddled against the dining-room door, uttering strange, plaintive sounds.

Fearing he might distress Nou-Nou, being a Tom, I carried him to the verandah, but he rushed back again, looking at me pleadingly with his golden eye.

I kept the door closed until the Vet had examined Nou-Nou.

'Hmm! She must have this injection, then…yes, I will see to this cut.'

When he had finished, he grinned at me: 'So, this is a kitten, did you say? Well, sorry to contradict you, but she is going to be a mother.'

'But she is so thin!'

'True. She is in bad shape. Starved, been in a fight, has a high temperature. That is why she refuses to eat. Still, not to worry. I know you will have her well again in no time.'

I told him about Miko's insistence to come in.

'Let him come, while I am here. Let us see what he is chafing about.'

When I opened the door, Miko rushed to Nou-Nou's side. To my amazement, he settled close beside her, then, with ever so gentle a touch, he began to lick her face.

Nou-Nou made no move to avoid his ministrations, instead, she closed her eyes as though totally exhausted.

We left them together.

'Let me see this budgie of yours, you saved, even when I had told you that you were wasting your time trying,' my Vet friend asked.

I laughed, and brought him to David Livingstone, so named because he had wandered off one day on a long walk (his wings having been clipped), to explore the world.

He had left the garden, managed to locate some nearby dust-bins, had clambered up one, and had promptly fallen in.

I had lamented his disappearance for hours, asking all and sundry, to search for my missing green budgie, who had been given to me as a birthday present, for, personally, I prefer to see birds, free and on the wing.

At eleven o'clock that night, there was a knock on my door, and there, a triumphant Night Watchman held out a filthy budgie to me: 'Missus, here he is. He was right at the bottom of one bin. Aie! He is dirty! Now, Missus, you are happy again?'

Another time, David Livingstone had decided to leave his familiar surroundings to explore the world yet again. This time, it was Rusty, the Doberman Pinscher, who came to me with green tail-feathers protruding from his mouth.

I had given such a piercing shriek that my father, who was admiring his roses at the time, blanched, and rushed to my side: 'What is it? What is it?' he had cried.

Another shriek, then: 'It is Rusty. He has eaten David Livingstone.'

A flood of tears. Papa had placed his arms about me. I would not be comforted.

I walked about the garden for hours, tears streaming down my cheeks.

Late that night, the neighbour's gardener, Andreas, appeared on my doorstep, white teeth flashing in a happy smile: 'Don't cry, Miss Gladys – here he is, David Livingstone!'

There he was, minus tail feathers, but otherwise fit and unrepentant.

My friend the Vet, now referred to the latest 'incident' with this Budgie-person.

The claws of David's right foot could not grasp his perch. I had discovered this one morning. Consequently, he fell ill.

Upon inspecting David, the Vet had told me ruefully: 'Nothing can be done for him, I am afraid. You could try rubbing some warm olive oil on the claw, but I doubt you will be able to save him.'

I had looked at my resolute explorer, eyes fixed unwaveringly on me. Cupping him in the palm of one hand, I had had a serious heart-to-heart talk with him, as he cocked his pretty head to one side, listening intently: 'You are such a brave little person,' I told him, in the special voice reserved for 'other-worldly' things. 'So brave, so adventurous! You do not want me to give up on you, I know that. I have rubbed the olive oil on your leg, but it has not done much good…I am going to try something quite different. If it works we will have won, if not, you will know that I have done my best for you.'

His bright, intelligent eyes regarded me steadily, then, ever so gently, he nibbled my finger:

'I trust you', he said to my heart, 'go ahead. Experiment away. I am all for it.'

And so I showed David, the bottle of Vidaylin vitamin drops which I had procured from my friend the Chemist, who, with an amused smile on his face, had listened to my latest epic on my animal colony, with his usual exemplary patience.

'I have phoned so many pet shops,' I had told Mr Lazer, 'but they all said that they could not help me. What do you think? I must try something. David Livingstone wants to go on exploring.'

Mr Lazer had laughed: 'So, he told you that, did he?' But his eyes were kind and, I thought, slightly misty.

He had taken a bottle from the shelf, and handed it to me: 'Try putting some Vidaylin into his drinking water. Can't hurt. They are only a vitamin supplement.'

Back home, I told my Budgie: 'This is going straight into your mouth, David.'

The intrepid explorer allowed me to open his beak and let some drops of Vidaylin fall into his mouth. He struggled a little, but I continued my treatment by giving him some water immediately afterwards, in case the Vitamins administered in its pure form, proved too strong.

Returned to his cage, David had closed his eyes. He was very weak.

When two days had passed without a change, I approached David the following morning with trepidation. What would I find?

Delight gripped me at what I saw.

There he was, my brave fellow, perched on his swing, claws firmly curled, eyes bright with zest for life. The small head turned towards me.

'David! You are better!'

I opened his door to receive the feathered treasure in my hands.

I wept with joy, as David danced from finger to finger, uttering strange sounds of ecstasy.

Now, my Vet friend, observed our explorer extraordinaire, as he raced up and down his rainbow-coloured ladder.

'Amazing! A few drops of Vidaylin. Who would have believed it? What a Vet you would have made. You also saved his mate. How did you know what to do? I still cannot understand all this.'

Mr Davis was referring to another incident, when David's light-of- love, 'Yellow Lady', developed hiccups which would not go away. My family looked on in mystified amazement as I carried the budgie against my heart for hours at an end, breathing into her mouth every few minutes. After four hours, her hiccuping ceased.

Where do we get these inspirations from?

Realm of Mystery! Surely from my Guardian Angel!

To return to Nou-Nou. She grew stronger with each passing hour, accepting food the next day, inspecting her new home, submitting to Miko's tender overtures, following me with a gaze which held within it an ancient mystery, a wisdom born of suffering nobly endured, nobly transformative.

When I held her against my heart, we went for walks in the garden with Miko walking alongside.

Beneath the generous shade of a golden – boughed Mimosa, we communed: 'I have known many dark times,' Nou-Nou told me, in heart-language, 'humans are rarely able to see us, you know, as being worthy of respect. I have observed them for a long time, hiding from them as much as I was able, for I found them, for the most part, to be rough and harsh of voice. Sometimes, driven by hunger, I had to brave their presence as I darted from cover to sample a scrap of discarded food. I have often been kicked, shouted at, pushed out of the way. And then, of course, there are the thugs of Cat-hood, who attack from nowhere…I am companion to solitude. I have tasted loneliness until now. I can embrace aloneness without fear…I have had to do many things to survive. A cat-person's life is like a shadow…learn to be very still – move only when you must – trust no one.'

I gently caressed her small head; 'You can trust me,' I told her, 'I will not harm you. I have known you forever. Your name sprang into my heart from a far long ago, like a forgotten melody surging back into the present. You are a precious fragment from my truest, deepest self. I love you.

The splendid eyes regarded me steadily. A cat-person sees through the façade, the persona, of a human…the spiritual X-rays pierce the outer layer to behold the quality of soul before it, or so it always seemed to me.

The silent scrutiny went on for some time, then, Nou-Nou put out a delicate paw and placed it on one cheek, stretching at the same time to give my other cheek a tender kiss-bite. Thus were our hearts linked in an unbreakable relationship.

From deep within her chest there issued a musical purring, sign that she was dancing with contentment inside her magical inner spaces.

Miko looked up, satisfied, then stretched out on my sandaled feet, relaxed, aware of all that was happening.

The breeze wafted perfume to our nostrils, the fragrance of my father's magnificent Rose-Garden, attired in glory, firing the surroundings with vivid scarlets, pale pinks, creams, yellows, tangerines. To the left, was an ancient Oak I loved, its large, gnarled branches bearing offering from mysterious realms, reminding me of the Sacred groves where holy rites were once performed in days of yore. It seemed to me that in this modern age of speed, technological breakthroughs, with its accent on scientific knowledge as being the newly deified authority to so many, that the art of reflection was fast becoming extinct…one must always be 'doing' things, so it seemed, 'achieving' this, and that. Introspection was for dreamers, poets, people who were somehow not 'with it'. If one mentioned the divine Essence of something, a barrier came up instantly. I have often been saddened by this reaction in so many, as though to look at the beauty of the Soul, was blasphemy.

There, holding Nou-Nou in my arms, feeling Miko's vibrations as he purred against my feet, surrounded my Nature's magnificence, I was transported to new heights. To someone observing the scene, it would appear that it revealed a woman and two cats. Not so. When there is harmony, Nature, animals and humans, combine to sing a mystical Song heard only by the Silence.

SNAPPY

....

Leaving the cat-people for a while, let me take the reader to the time when Snappy entered our lives. He was a Maltese poodle, creamy-white in colour, with buff and tan markings. His eyes were superb. They were a clear, golden, hazel-brown.

I went to the S.P.C.A. to select a dog for my son's birthday. When however, I found myself looking at all the abandoned animals pressing their faces eagerly against the fence, as though calling: 'Take me! Take me!' I could not bear it a moment longer. I turned, hurried away, tears sliding down my cheeks.

Back in the office, an embarrassed-looking official handed me a tissue.

'I cannot. I just cannot,' I told him, 'You choose. Give me the most unhappy animal you have. Please.'

'Well, there is a little chap who came here with his sister, She was adopted, you know, taken – but, well, he is moping for her, and hasn't eaten for days. He is a sad little fellow.'

'I will take him.'

Blue eyes regarded me with a surprised look in them: 'Don't you want to look at him first, Madam?'

'No. That won't be necessary. I will take him home now.'

And so it was that Snappy was carried to my car where I had placed a newly-bought basket and brightly-coloured cushion. Without uttering a bark, he lowered his head on to his paws, brown eyes overflowing with a sorrow which streamed into my own heart.

As I drove homewards, I conversed with him: 'You are going to be a birthday gift, so you must not be sad. We will make you so welcome in our home – you will see! You will learn to laugh again, dance again, I promise – please don't look so sad!'

Once home, I brought Snappy inside, straight into the bathroom.

Tying my apron about my waist, I proceeded to give Snappy a thorough shampoo, somewhat alarmed at the lack of interest this dog-person showed for this task. He appeared to be in a catatonic state, standing absolutely still, evincing no emotion at lather, water, conditioning, drying, and brushing.

He proved me wrong.

Suddenly, he made his move.

Like a flash, he was out of the bathtub, a creamy blur. Uttering my usual shriek of dismay whenever I am horrified, I raced after my son's birthday present. Down the street we went, a beautiful flow of grace, and a woman pounding behind in apron and high heels, uttering cries of: 'Stop him! Stop him!' to all those who gaped in astonishment at the sight.

Needless to say, no one made the slightest move.

Like pillars of salt, they watched the drama enacted in their midst, or was it, comedy?

Snappy continued running. I would not give up.

Eventually, he stopped beside a Bus Terminal, panting, with a pink tongue hanging to one side of his mouth.

I pounced on him, bundled him up in my apron, trudged back home as irate humans are wont to do, keeping my tongue silent inside my mouth, but this does not mean that I was not mentally telling Snappy what I thought of his Great-escape act.

Back inside, I locked the doors, limped into the kitchen to make myself a well-earned cup of tea.

Snappy sat on his haunches, watching me.

I placed some water in front of him.

He did not hesitate. Down it went, in great gulps.

Whilst the tea brewed, I prepared some food for my new friend.

To my delight it disappeared as well.

So far, so good!

I sipped my tea, decided I should reward myself with a biscuit.

Snappy cocked an ear, sniffed the air, looked at me: 'Are you not going to share?'

I stared: 'What! You want some of my biscuit after the tricked you played on me?'?'

'Don't see why not. I have a right to express my feelings you know.....If you knew what I have been through.....'

I knelt down beside him, held him tight.

The bond was established. Our hearts were wedded.

Snappy reacted very strangely to the first time we put him on a lead. He turned a somersault, then lay on his back, refusing to turn over.

Somehow, that lead must have had associations for him with being taken to the animal Shelter.

Apart from that one 'revolt', Snappy never looked back.

He used to ride in the back of our car when we went to the Drive-in Cinema, loved to put his face out of the window as the car's speed forced fresh air in his direction. His leaping, bounding body was grace in motion as he tore along green fields with my son.

Gone was the sorrowful look, instead, joy radiated from him.

At story-time, he listened with cocked ears to the rise and fall of my voice, as intently as did my son, four brown eyes resting on my face.

He became my shadow, dogging my footsteps throughout the day, alert for strange footsteps, growling deeply in his throat if anyone came to the door.

When I went on holiday with my family, I entrusted him to my maternal aunt Miriam, knowing he would be well cared for.

Upon our return, I was told that he managed to bolt out of the door one day, to my aunt's utter dismay. He had disappeared into the night. Frantic, knowing how much Snappy was loved, my aunt sent out reinforcements to search for this very special dog-person, but to no avail. No trace of him could be found. Then, the telephone rang. It was a call from my neighbour. She told my aunt that Snappy was lying in front of our front door. A car was dispatched forthwith, and Snappy was once again in her care.

One Sunday morning, my parents came on a visit. My brother Francis was with them, and I asked him to walk a short distance to the shop to get some milk. My son, who was then six years old, went with him, with Snappy at his heels.

Suddenly, disaster. A big collie rushed out of an open gate, charging straight for Snappy. My son picked up his dog to protect him. The collie lunged. There was a blur of motion, the collie's teeth ripping my son's left cheek, just below the eye.

Francis my brother, came running home, carrying Guillaume.

My shriek rang out at sight of my son's bloody visage.

In no time at all we were at the Hospital, where the doctor put stitches into the ugly gash caused by the collie's teeth.

That night, Snappy kept vigil with me, as we watched over Guillaume. I was afraid the bed linen might snag on the stitches, so I spent hours observing him.

It had been a very brave thing to do, this protecting Snappy. I was very proud of my son, but also very concerned that his scars would be ugly. I need not have worried. They became less visible with the passage of years, for, like all mothers, I was anxious that the beauty of my child remain unmarred.

RUSTY

....

Kalamazoo, the African gardener, was a unique personality.

He appeared one afternoon, like an apparition from another planet.

His feet were encased in old sandals, his trousers were baggy, too large, too long, held together with a thick cord. Over his once-white shirt was a thread-bare jacket of indeterminable colour, decorated by jagged tears of varying sizes. Some pretty flowers peeped forth from these strange cloth 'vases'.

The face was beautiful. The eyes lustrous, the teeth an immaculate white. His smile was bewitching, lighting up his features so that the kindliness of expression which Kalamazoo habitually wore, was heightened to a sort of glow, a certain radiance.

About his white hair he wore a head-band made of a dark material on which had been affixed Coca-Cola caps, buttons of different colours and sizes, finishing with an astonishing array of bright flowers.

As I stood, riveted by this fascinating person, he flashed me his magnificent smile: 'I am Kalamazoo. I want work. I will take out your weeds for you – you have sooooo much!'

With this, he made a graceful gesture with both arms outspread, as though about to take flight.

I nodded, too astonished to speak.

Snappy trotted after Kalamazoo, interested and curious.

I went into the kitchen to prepare tea for my unexpected visitor. I made some sandwiches.

When I emerged into the sunlight, tray in hand, I gasped at what I saw.

Kalamazoo was calmly uprooting my flowers!

'Stop! Stop!'

The smile flashed in my direction. The eyes alighted on the tray. The smile grew broader.

'Ah. Good! Kalamazoo is hongry!'

'You are pulling out my flowers instead of taking out the weeds,' I protested.

The old man sat back on his heels, studied the garden with its bright blooms, uprooted.

'Ah! Not good. Kalamazoo is old. Eyes are not working properly.'

Suddenly, my heart received a slap: 'How dare you,' spoke my Inner voice, 'how dare you. This old man could be your grandfather. He should be seated in the shade somewhere, not toiling on hands and knees in your garden. Desist this minute. Wake up!'

To the surprise of the old Zulu, I made him stop work, brought him inside, placed the tea and sandwiches before him, and watched him tuck in.

I learnt that he had nowhere to sleep, that he went from house to house seeking light work.

From that day on, Kalamazoo slept in the garage, had breakfast and dinner at our place. At the crack of dawn a voice would call: 'Picannin, Picannin (young one), wake up! Tell your mother, Kalamazoo is very hongry...'

Soon, Guillaume would exit our kitchen carrying our guest's breakfast.

One day, a delegation visited me comprised of women who lived in the same street. They complained about the loud singing of the itinerant. This drunken singing, they said, was causing a disturbance.

'He is often drunk,' one woman stated.

'You must stop feeding him, then, he will move on,' advised another.

'If you do not do as we ask, we will tell the police that he is disturbing our peace and quiet,' threatened a young lady.

I gave them a steely look: 'And to think you call yourselves, Christians! Well, I have this to say to you. Kalamazoo is one of our household. If he disturbs you when he is tipsy, that is just too bad! Far from being a nuisance, he is a marvellous person, full of laughter, full of fun, with no malice towards anyone. I would rather listen to his singing, than have to put up with the dreadful racket your youngsters set loose on this neighbourhood when you hold party sessions. As for the police, by all means inform them that I am caring for an old man who is as poor as a church-mouse, and who has no family of his own. That is surely a terrible crime I am committing.

One by one, the women left. They never bothered me again.

One day, Kalamazoo died whilst visiting a friend at Alexandra Township. He had been with us seven years. When the police notified me, we made arrangements for Kalamazoo to have a fine funeral.

It had been on one sunny afternoon, when Kalamazoo had dropped in for a chat, tea and biscuits, that Snappy had begun to bark furiously.

Upon investigating the cause, I saw a beautiful Doberman Pinscher outside my gate.

My sister's car drew up just at that moment. Pretty as a picture, Jacqueline stepped out, her eyes widening at sight of the Doberman.

'Where did he come from?' she called out.

'I have no idea,' I replied.

Jackie sidled past the Doberman, then quickly closed the gate behind her. We both studied him. Snappy had ceased his barking.

Kalamazoo had said: 'He is hongry!'

Rushing into the kitchen, I took a pound of sausages from the refrigerator, proffered them to the Doberman. With great gulps, he downed the meat.

'He is starving!' Jackie declared.

We went inside to partake of some refreshment, and to chat.

When Jackie was leaving, we found the Doberman had not stirred from the gate.

He was very handsome, with a refined, intelligent expression on his tan and black face. In the afternoon sunshine, his eyes gleamed like honey.

'Papa and maman have no dog,' Jackie mused, 'I will take him to them now. It is obvious he has been abandoned.'

Rusty found a home with our parents.

When I moved to their double-storey dwelling some time later, Rusty and Snappy became fast friends. The tall Doberman with his long, purposeful stride, the elegant, powerful protector of the property, contrasted with the fluffy, creamy glamour of the Maltese poodle, who nevertheless gave warning barks to would-be trespassers, trying to do his bit as guard-dog.

Miko and Nou-Nou were wary of both dogs, sensing that good behaviour on the latter's part was only a temporary truce due to my restraining presence.

I concentrated mainly on my writing in those days, spending many hours on the veranda upstairs. It afforded me a view of the Bowling Club's sweeping lawns across the road from our house, a grandstand opportunity to watch a colony of Weaver birds at their nest-building to my right, as well as being a great vantage point for observing our pets as they wandered about in the garden.

When relaxing from my writing, I took note of a certain activity as the Weaver birds flew past in purposeful and regular patterns. One in particular, I grew to recognize because of distinctive markings on his plumage. So beautiful, so graceful was he, that I named him 'Mr Delightful.'

Sometimes, he would perch on the nearby apple tree, to watch my 'weaving' of words on paper.

At tea-time, I scattered some biscuit crumbs for my angel-bird. Timidly at first, then, with growing confidence, Mr Delightful pecked daintily at these tit-bits, bright eyes on me as he savoured his break from work.

'Do you think your lady-love will approve of your home this time!' I asked him. 'I saw her turn up her beak at your last effort.'

His eyes flashed a reply: 'One can only keep trying. Must go now, can't fall behind with the task.'

Now, it was Rusty's turn to taste some biscuits. I caressed his noble head after he had eaten. He placed it on my lap, his eyes fixed unwaveringly on me as quivers of happiness rippled across his frame, vibrating like the strings of a harp which have known delicate touch.

Animals are very wise. Rusty knew I loved him.

I have always thought it strange why some humans believe themselves to possess attributes which they deny to animals. So often I have heard the words: 'An animal is not a human being endowed with intelligence. You are far too sentimental for your own good. It is a known fact that animals have no souls. Your attitude is more that of a mystic...' And what, 'would be my riposte,' is wrong with that? Wordsworth could describe flowers as 'A host of golden daffodils. William Blake wrote: "See Heaven in a grain of sand," why then, should I not see everything 'crowned in Divine Glory?'

Rusty had endured much. Humans had not been kind to him. From deep within his inner landscapes there surfaced the sufferings he had been through, the bewilderment of rejection, of abandonment, the loneliness and dread of having been cast out into a hostile, alien environment. Sorrow still stood, like a sentinel on the outposts of his being, but gradually, Rusty was learning to trust again, to hope again, above all, to love again.

I had placed a rug on a settee nearby, for Rusty to sprawl on. It was his special place when he was relaxing from patrol duty, for Rusty was ever on the alert, ears pricked for the slightest hostile move or noise.

He had leapt to my defence one day, when I had found myself alone in the big house. Intent on my writing, I had been unaware of the quiet footsteps on the stairs, nor did I take any notice when both Snappy and rusty growled.

Suddenly, there was a blur of motion as Rusty launched himself through the air, straight at the African who had appeared so stealthily. Rusty's awesome teeth ripped through the intruder's shirt, then my fingers curled about is collar.

'Down, Rusty, down!' I ordered.

Still baring his teeth, growling ominously, Rusty obeyed, even as I took stock of the man before me.

'Who are you? What do you want?' I enquired, 'you are very lucky I was here, otherwise my dog would have hurt you.'

Without a word, the African bolted, his feet barely touching the steps. His departure sounded like castanets.

I watched his burly frame race up the driveway, his arms moving like pistons, head bent low into his chest as if he wanted to bury the sight of the furious Doberman.

At that moment, Tatti Dlomo our gardener, hurried into view, a worried look on his face. In his hand he held a broom: 'Miss Gladys, I saw that tsotsi (bandit), run away. He came through the kitchen door when I went to my room. I saw somebody coming inside – but I was too late. Aie! Miss Gladys, I must not leave the door open again.'

I told him about Rusty's 'calling card'. Tatti was delighted, a big grin spreading from ear to ear, eyes alight with glee.

Tatti was in his early twenties. He had been with my parents for five years before I moved in.

Slim, wiry in build, Tatti had a handsome face. His home was in Natal, where his mother and her other children lived on a small farm. Every month Tatti sent his family, part of his wages.

Tatti and I developed a special relationship which began when I stopped him from pouring hot water over ants whilst he was cleaning out the back steps.

'You may use cold water, Tatti,' I had told him, 'never hot water. Let me show you something. Come inside.'

Wonderingly, the young man had seated himself at my kitchen table. I brought him one of my Encyclopaedias, which I proceeded to open until I found the page I sought.

'Here, look at this. This is a photograph of ants. See, they are choosing a king.'

White teeth flashed, a look of incredulity came over the young Zulu's face: 'Aie! Miss Gladys'.

'I am not telling a lie,' I assured him, 'ants are very intelligent. Listen, I will read this to you.'

Time passed. Tatti's face was a study. Emotions chased themselves across his features.

'And here is a story relating how, many ants were killed by passing trains as they crawled across some rail-tracks. Then, the ants found another way across, by digging a way underneath the rails. So, you see, Tatti, how very clever ants are. That is why it is a shame to kill them when it is not necessary. Ants can swim. All you have to do is throw cold water on the outside steps – the ants will be taken by the water to the ground below – then, they hurry away to their homes. They can live, and you are free of doing them harm.'

Tatti's finger traced the outline of the photograph on the glossy page. A tender expression softened his features, so that the appeared younger, more vulnerable.

'How! A king! They have soldiers, these ant-people?'

From that time one, we used to chat about life in general. I bought Tatti exercise books, taught him some Arithmetic, how to read and write. His conversion to animal-love continued. I stopped him killing birds with his catapult, showing him superb photos in books, reading to him about their habits, their cleverness, their migratory trails, finishing with: 'And why do you think Artists give Angels, wings? Because birds are like our hearts which want to sing and dance in the sky – when we are happy, it is as though our hearts have wings – and up, up, we fly, into a wonderful, free place, where laughter lives – up there, where the Rainbow shines! God created birds to give us something beautiful to behold and listen to, so that when we are sad, a bird flying through the air brings peace to our hearts...Tatti, you must not harm anything if you can help it. To be kind to all, is to be a true lover of God, and you tell me you always keep your Bible by your bed.'

'Aie! Miss Gladys, you make my heart think!'

With quiet steps Tatti walked away, musing.

One morning, he came to me, carrying a huge pigeon.

'Miss Gladys, that boy next door, he did shoot this bird with his gun. I saw him. I bring him to you, this poor, hurt fellow'.

I saw the blood steadily dripping from the right wing.'

'I must get the Vet,' I told Tatti. 'Thank you for bringing him to me. I am proud of you.'

My friend, Mr Davis, came as soon as he was able. He examined the bird, clipped part of the hurt wing, then told me: 'Keep him in this cage for precisely ten days, then, let him take wing. If he does not fly, he will have to be put down. Let us hope for the best.'

When the tenth day dawned, Tatti accompanied me into the tennis court, closing the gate firmly behind us to keep out our cat and dog colony.

I had named our patient, Ramana, after Bhagavan Sri Ramana Maharshi, the Sage.

As the sun picked out the glossy marvel of the bird's feathers, I kissed him on the head, held my hands up, then tossed the pigeon upwards: 'Fly, Ramana, fly,' I called out, my heart trembling with apprehension.

I need not have worried. The wonderful wings opened bravely, a mighty surge, the head lifted, then, Ramana was away, over the wire – fence. Up, up, into the fragrant morn.

Tatti and I smiled at each other in huge delight.

With the passage of time, Tatti matured, as did our relationship.

When on his day-off, one Saturday, Tatti was attacked by some tsotsis (bandits), in Hillbrow, he asked the police who were quickly on the scene, to 'fetch Miss Gladys.' He refused to go into the ambulance before I arrived. I received the phone call, and rushed to the scene, finding him seated on the grassy verge by the road, bleeding profusely from a deep gash in his right thigh. The thugs had demanded him to give them his expensive watch. When Tatti refused, one of them had stabbed him viciously.

Triumph overrode the pain in his eyes: 'I did not let them take my watch, Miss Gladys.'

'You were very brave, Tatti,' was my response, before the ambulance doors closed on us.

My experience with Tatti Dlomo proved to me that when a heart is taught kindness, it responds in spontaneous fashion, for compassion is the Sleeping Beauty who wakens with a kiss...to tenderness and love. There are, of course, hearts cloaked in deep darkness. They perform dark deeds which are evil, but they must be in our prayers, for 'there, but for the Grace of God, go I.'

Throughout the years we were together, Tatti and I shared many interesting and enriching experiences.

LI - LI and SITA

My uncle Robert, who was a Chevalier of the Legion of Honour, told me a story about a Chimpanzee called Charlotte who had been adopted by his friends in French Equatorial Africa, Mr and Mrs Wewig.

Charlotte had been orphaned at an early age, but fortunately for her, she had stolen the hearts of the elderly French couple to such an extent that they loved her like the child they had never had.

She proved to very close to a human child, as she was incredibly intelligent, loving, and resourceful.

Hidden in the luxuriant foliage of her favourite trees, Charlotte watched the neighbours' 'activities with live interest, registering where there emanated 'hostile' elements as opposed to 'kindlier' vibrations.

One lady in particular, had taken an instant dislike to the Wewig's precocious animal-child, telling all and sundry, that it was unwholesome to love a monkey, allow her to live in your home, play an active role in your life, and, above all, incite feelings of affection.

Charlotte's intuition was unerring regarding this neighbour. She remembered, as animals are wont to do, in her heart-diary, every insult this woman hurled at her, every abusive gesture she made in her direction. Wise and as patient as the forest in which she loved to roam, Charlotte bided her time.

One day, she made her move.

The neighbour-with-nasty- vibrations, had baked a cake for her child's birthday.

Eyes as bright as buttons, observed the lady icing her cake, decorating it with elaborate designs, complete with floral display of marzipan.

The apron was whipped off, the stout woman sallied forth from the kitchen, cheeks ruddy from her culinary exertions.

Charlotte slipped through the window, like a shadow cast on a wall. In her hand was a bottle of ink.

With great deliberation she emptied the blue-black contents over the birthday cake, then, to add insult to injury, she placed one hand over the ink after which she wiped it on the tablecloth.

Satisfied, Charlotte went home. Years of insults had been repaid. Content, the Chimpanzee climbed a tree, swung her legs in graceful movement, settled against the solid, warm bole of her favourite leafy-friend, waiting for the shouting to begin. When it did, she bared her teeth in a delighted grin.

On another occasion, a guest entered the Wewig's bathroom. Leaving her bed, (Charlotte slept in her very own bed), she turned the key in the bathroom door, slipped the key under her pillow, then closed her eyes as though fast asleep.

The guest rattled the door handle, called out. His hosts rushed to the spot, could not find the key, hunted for it.

'It must be Charlotte!' Madame Wewig told her husband.

They looked down at their sleeping cherub. Sensing their displeasure, Charlotte kept her eyes closed, gently eased the key from under the pillow, and held it out to her human parents.

Nou-Nou was about to become a mother. I had placed a basket in readiness for this eventful occasion, close to my bed, keeping an anxious eye on the mother-to-be.

To my surprise, Nou-Nou leaped on to my bed, gave me a golden look of love, then laid her head on my lap. I called out to my son, Guillaume, to bring me some towels, for it was obvious that Nou-Nou wanted me to be near.

We placed a cushion and towels under Nou-Nou, and Guillaume stood by the bed, eyes full of concern.

I stroked Nou-Nou's gleaming fur. The split on her nose had never completely closed, but to me, she was very beautiful. She had a soul quality I could not fail to recognize, which evoked the deepest love and tenderness. There was an uninterrupted flow of something indefinable which bordered on the awesome mysteriousness of Life itself, between us. Even now, as I try to define what heart-language we spoke, words fail me miserably. Looking into Nou-Nou's eyes was like looking at starlight, like soaking in the tranquillity and peace of a tropical lagoon where turquoise waters sing, the breezes dance on palm fronds, where sands sight with pure contentment at the kiss of sun and wave. Nou-Nou brought magic into my life!

As her labour progressed, she looked deep into my yes, moaning as the contractions grew stronger. I spoke to her in low tones, encouraging her.

Hours passed. By now, Nou-Nou was exhausted. The six bundles squirming about her body had drained her energies.

Guillaume's eyes were wet, but he gave me a delighted grin, as we both surveyed our enlarged family whom we had placed in the basket.

We opened the door to admit Miko, who had been waiting patiently nearby, like a sentry on duty. Once again, I was struck by the deep affection which he displayed towards Nou-Nou, and an attentiveness, tempered by a tenderness which was touching.

Now, he surveyed mother and kittens with his one golden eye, then, gently, he began to lick Nou-Nou's fine head. From his throat came a steady purring, as though conveying his pride and congratulations. He then took up a position beside the basket, never stirring from the spot till morning.

I recalled a friend of mine, telling me how she had watched a strange sight once, in the Congo, when she was a young girl. On a low wall in their garden lay an emaciated, not so young, cat. She had given birth to two kittens, but was too exhausted to push the last baby out. Suddenly, a Tom came to her aid. Ever so delicately, he took the emerging kitten into his mouth, then edged it out with slow, determined movement, until the kitten flopped on to the wall. He carried on with his ministrations until the mother had regained her strength enough to place her little ones in a safe place.

Watching Miko's behaviour with Nou-Nou, I marvelled at how little we humans really know about our animal brethren.

Our six kittens were a delight, but the time came, when I had to find homes for four of them. We were keeping two.

Guillaume promptly took the loveliest, long-haired, misty-grey one, called Lakshmi.

'It is not right to keep Nou-Nou's most glamorous child,' I told him gently, 'we must give them all the same chance, don't you agree?'

My son's expressive brown eyes met mine. Tears were not far away, but his innate fairness made him nod his head. I took him into my arms.

Of course, Lakshmi was the first to find a home, as were the three other 'pretty ones.' We kept a thin, black kitten whom we called Sita, and her brother, whose grey fur was dabbled with white. He was named Li - Li.

True, Sita was scrawny, possessed no silky, long coat. Her face was tiny, but her eyes were like her mother's, they spoke of mysterious depths. She followed me about like a shadow, observing me for hours at an end, caressing me with her looks of love.

Li- Li was brave, bold, gentle. He and his sister were inseparable. Sleeping with paws about each other, licking with great energy, the ears, face, body, of the other, their small pink tongues flicking away like an industrious housewife with her duster.

The house in which we lived was very spacious, one of those old-fashioned buildings where ceilings are high, the rooms of a generous size.

My parents and my brother Francis, occupied the ground floor, where we would repair at night, to have coffee and spend some time together.

One night, my brother Francis who had played tennis at Wimbledon, told us that three famous tennis players were coming to play at Ellis Park in a Championship, and that he had offered to put them up for a few days.

My parents were delighted. The conversation became animated as plans were made for the visit. Papa decided to have our drive-way resurfaced entirely.

Accordingly, lorries found their way to our house, disgorging their contents under papa's sharp eyes.

Eventually all was in readiness. The driveway looked superb. The interior of our home sparkled, vases displayed fragrant bouquets, crystal glasses held the honey-shaded joy of Champagne, as our guests were welcomed in style.

Life is filled with the unexpected.

It materialised in the form of fleas. They arrived like one of the plagues of Egypt, hopping, skipping, biting…

Francis was horrified, my parents, mortified.

My father stood on his bed, clad in his pyjamas when I entered the room the next morning. He held a pair of trousers in his hand, which he was shaking so vigorously, that I burst out laughing: 'Papa, what are you doing?'

A fierce glare was directed at me; 'This is no laughing matter! I am making sure there are no fleas in my clothes before I put them on. We must find out where all these fleas are coming from, before our guests are further inconvenienced.'

My laughter would not subside: 'But papa, why are you standing on your bed? Fleas can jump.'

'Do you think I don't know that?' came the irritated reply. 'I just feel safer from them up here.'

Maman came in at that moment, and she joined in my laughter.

Papa was not amused.

When we sat around the breakfast-table, papa said: 'These pests must be coming from your cats.'

'That is not possible,' I answered, 'there are no fleas upstairs. I slept like an angel. It is only downstairs that they are hopping about everywhere – they must be coming from outside.'

Papa suddenly stood up: 'The driveway. That's the explanation!'

We followed him outside. We saw tiny fleas all along the driveway.

The telephone wires hummed with papa's ire. Some time later, the lorries were back again, this time, taking back the new surface they had covered our driveway with. A man appeared at the front door, his face pink with embarrassment as he explained that, quite by accident, there were sand-fleas in the 'new material' and so forth, and so forth.

Papa made no comment, but exacted a guarantee from the 'Company' that there would be no more fleas on his property by nightfall.

By the time our tennis guests returned, the crisis was over. They slept undisturbed, to the great relief of my father in particular, whose idea it had been in the first place, to have a brand-new driveway.

==================

Our neighbour next door, had a teenage son who was very cruel towards animals. We had had an experience of his callousness with the shooting of the pigeon. What we did not know was that he set traps for our cats.

Li - Li was the unfortunate victim, but I did not detect his plight straight away.

I had noticed that Li - Li's manner was strange as he came into the kitchen. He would not eat or drink, but stared at me, hunching up his body. When I stroked him under the chin, I let out a piercing shriek, the urgency of which, sent my brother Francis flying up the stairs.

I told him: 'Li - Li has a wire round his throat. I can't get it off!'

Francis's strong fingers sought, located and pulled at the awful wire-necklace. The spring holding it in place, snapped. The wire fell away.

I gathered Li - Li into my arms, weeping at the horror of it. A big kiss of thanks for my brother, then I took Li - Li to my room, where I placed him on my pillow.

He was in pain, could barely swallow. It was too late in the night to call my Vet friend so I soaked some cotton wool in cool water, then let it fall, drop by drop, on to LI - Li's tongue.

Green eyes gazed at me piteously, gratefully! That night, Li - Li kept his head on my pillow. Now and again, I would use the cotton wool to give him water. He never stirred, conserving his energies, swallowing with difficulty.

When Dr Davis examined the wounded throat, the next day, he gave Li - Li an antibiotic, and then a pain-killer. He then accompanied me to our neighbour's house, where he told the parents of this teenager that he would notify the police about the incident. He then told the youth to bring him all the other traps which he had made.

Blazing defiance, nevertheless the youth complied.

I told him in no uncertain words what would happen to him if he tormented any other animal.

When I parted from my Vet-friend, he said: 'Let us hope that that scoundrel has no other traps.'

Some months later, this same youth stabbed one of my cats, named Mimi. She died with the knife still protruding from her small body. This lad delighted in shooting birds, and before he left our neighbourhood for ever, he sent his four Alsatians into their chicken house to destroy the hens. He was one of the cruellest young men I have ever met.

Hell is indeed where Love is not.

* * * * * * * * * * * * *

The Glory And The Dream

. . . .

'I was often unable to think of external things as having external existence, and I communed with all I saw as something not apart from but inherent in my own nature.'

- (William Wordsworth)

There are 'happenings' which appear to be trivial, of no special significance or importance, yet their 'vividness' linger on, as the fragrance of roses cling to the tresses of the breeze.

I recall a stroll along a beach one summer morning. In holiday mood, I enjoyed the leisure of allowing mind and body to float on bubbles of contentment...a hand touched my arm. Started, I turned to see an Indian fisherman at my side, a friendly smile on his face. He lifted his hands to show me the crab he held.

'Madam, this is a big one. Make a fine meal!'

A surprised look came over his face, at my sudden recoil.

'No, no, thank you.'

I moved away hurriedly, loathe to look again at the struggling creature. There was no need to tell the man that I was a vegetarian.

Sensing his gaze on me, I turned to give him a friendly wave, lest my abrupt departure had caused offence.

Upon my return to that strip of beach some time later, the same fisherman waved me over. I walked to where he stood, somewhat apprehensively, as I did not relish being offered another unfortunate creature to titillate my palate. Sure enough, there, on the warm, golden sands, was a large fish, its mouth opening and closing convulsively.

'Madam, this is a wonderful fellow! See how fat he is.'

To me, this was no fish on the beach. It was poor, struggling humanity.

'Can I buy it?' I asked quickly, tears misting my sight, heart hurting.

He nodded, again, the same look of surprise creeping into his gaze.

Leaning down, I swooped up the fish in both hands, ran towards the sea, splashed into the cool water, not checking my flight until the waves reached my shoulders, then, I opened my hands and let the fish go. His body formed an arc, like a rainbow, before falling into its life-sustaining element.

And so it is with us, I said to the departing silver miracle. Man is that fish. We struggle and agonize because we have left our true element, which is the Spiritual Realm. In vain, we writhe and gasp, caught in the net of materialism, held fast by desire, greed, avarice.........ignorance is our captor.

Caught in my mood of reverie, I stood there quite a while, seeing in my mind's eye, the liberated fish revelling in his escape, body in perfect rhythm with its element, dancing its dance of joy as it flew across the sea-scape.

'Free! Free!' sang the wind. My heart sang also.

I turned, walked out of the sea.

The fisherman awaited me, cap in hand.

'You must be paid your price for the fish I have taken,' I told him.

When this had been taken care of, there was a shifting from one leg to another by the Indian fisherman in apparent timidity, which was in marked contrast to the extrovert who had drawn my attention to himself, twice.

I took in the trousers rolled up to the knees, the brown short-sleeved shirt, wiry arms and legs, the thick, black hair ruffled by the wind, noted the long dark lashes which framed lustrous eyes. The strong hands twisted his cloth cap.

'I am Joseph. Please, remember me.'

I smiled, waiting for his next words.

'Madam, I will never forget you. This day something very great has happened...you bought my fish, not to sell it, not to cook it, but – to give it back to God!'

It was my turn to be surprised. How could this stranger have possibly known my inner feelings?

We stood there, staring at one another, oblivious of the curious gaze of passers-by.

I took his hands in mine: 'I promise to remember you, Joseph,' I said.

He grasped my fingers tightly: 'I will go to the Mosque to give thanks for this day. This fishing rod, I will put away. You have spoken to my heart this day, Madam. To pay me money, then to return to God His own creature.'

I told him: 'Joseph, there is one thing I should like you to do for me. When you catch a fish, strike it quickly, so that it does not suffer. Sometimes, it is necessary to fish for a living, but there is no need to be cruel. A quick death for your catch, is all I ask of you.'

Joseph regarded me with a look of awe, as though his gaze perceived the compassion veiled by my words.

'I will do as you say,' he told me, 'never, never, can I forget you!'

And so we parted, Joseph and I. Yet, even as I write, he stands before me, earnest, sincere, candid as a child, surely one who was pure of heart. He had even dared to show me his tears. Rare privilege indeed!

Another vivid 'happening' took place at a small dorp (village), in the Cape province in South Africa, where I had gone, to be alone with myself at a crisis period of my life.

I caught my breath sharply: 'What are you going to do with these goats?' I heard myself asking.

I had left my money at the Hotel, upon the advice of the Manager, and was walking along the town's main street, on my first exploration of the place, when I came upon a young African of about twelve years old, bare-footed, clad in khaki shirt and shorts, holding the ropes to which two goats were tied.

Suddenly, everything around me retreated into the background. The golden eyes of the goats were so anguished, so filled with sadness, that my heart raced with sympathy.

Here before me, was revealed the sorrow of the world. In those eyes, I saw such suffering! The cheeky-faced picannin (youngster) replied in Afrikaans: 'On sal hulle moor!' (we will murder them).

Something came over me, a force took over, powerful and fiery: 'No! I will buy them from you. Please wait here, I will come back with the money.'

I was the spectator in a curious way, and yet I was also the creature who dashed across the street to enter a Trading Store where an astonished Asian heard me blurt out: 'Is there and S.P.C.A. here!'

'No,' he replied.

I ran out, raced along the pavement, past a Bakery, a Butchery, into a Bank, straight up the stairs, past some counters, stopping only to knock at the door which sign read: 'Manager'.

'Come in,' said a voice.

I sped towards the Manager, the owner of the voice: 'I do not have time to explain. Can you let me have fifty Rands? I am staying at the Hotel. I have left my money there. I must have this sum straight away. It is a question of life and death. I will sign a receipt for it, of course, and you can ring the Hotel to check whether they are holding monies for me.'

Too amazed to ask questions, the Manager made a call, then handed me some notes, watched me sign the receipt for same, then saw me disappear like a flash.

He was still looking bemused when I returned soon after, shaking with sobs. Unable to speak, I held out the notes he had given me.

'My dear Madam, what is wrong? Please, sit down.'

I allowed myself to be shepherded to a comfortable chair where I collapsed, in tears.

My personal problems were linked with the sorrow I had seen in the eyes of the animals; as though clasped in each others' arms, we had tumbled down into the Abyss of Pain...my heart wept for the poor goats who were to be ritually slaughtered - a slow, cruel death! I had been too late. The African lad had no doubt disbelieved that I would return with the money, and had simply disappeared.

I was inconsolable.

A hand took mine, a voice said: 'Please try to drink this tea. It will do you good.'

I looked up into the concerned face of the Bank Manager who was leaning over me, proffering a cup.

It was some time before I could drink.. Once I had downed the hot liquid, the storm overtook me again. It was too much!

I said, haltingly: 'I – could not – save them. I – was – too late.'

The Manager had seated himself behind his desk. He fixed his eyes on me, wonderingly: 'Who could you not save, madam?'

'My goats.'

Shocked rigid, the Manager sat bolt upright; 'Goats, madam?'

'Yes. You see, I was walking along the street. I only arrived yesterday afternoon, and suddenly, I saw this picannin with the two goats. He told me they were to be murdered, so I wanted to buy them from him, but he did not wait for me to return. So, I could not save them. They will die a horrible death.'

'But what would you have done with these goats, madam?'

'There is a Vet in the town, is there not?'

'Yes, but…'

'Well, I would have asked him to either give them to a farmer, or put them down with an injection. The important thing, for me, was to save them from pain.'

The Manager was quite speechless.

My tears began to flow again, as I imagined the terror and pain which would come to the poor goats, before merciful death came to release them.

I broke out passionately: 'There is no need at all for cruelty. Why must animals suffer so? Is it not enough to take away their lives, without inflicting agony on them as well? Look at what we so-called civilized beings are doing in abattoirs? In this enlightened, so-advanced, technological success-story of ours, why is there no humane method of killing animals for food? Do you mean to tell me that our scientists cannot find some sleeping pills or powders, to give to these animals so that their hearts just cease beating? A substance could be introduced into their drinking water, or an injection given, whilst they eat quietly. It is a fact that fear, pain, enters the bloodstream, so that when humans inflict suffering on the animals they are having slaughtered, they then imbibe these humours when they in turn consume their flesh. Why not be humane, and truly civilized? We treat animals as barbarians do!'

Another cup of tea found its way into my hand.

The Manager told me: 'Please, go on. I want to hear more. You have such fire, and so many tears…I never thought one could weep like this over animals.'

A sodden tissue was replaced by a dry one.

'What is an animal?'

'I beg your pardon?'

'I asked a simple question. What do you understand is meant by the word, animal?'

The man made a pyramid with his fingers, then, collapsed them as though deciding to break down his facades as well. A thoughtful expression appeared on his face; 'An animal belongs to a species below man. It is endowed with a certain intelligence, instincts. It cannot reason, but it possesses emotions as we do.....that is about it!'

'Are you a Christian, Mr...'

'Actually, am a Catholic.'

'Therefore, you believe in a Being Whose attributes are, Omniscience, Omnipotence, and Omnipresence.'

'Correct.'

'It is the Omnipresence I should like to draw your attention to, because it signifies that the Divine is also present in animals, in those goats, for instance, I so wanted to save.'

The Manager stood up, crossed his arms, peered across the room at me with sharp alertness, and renewed interest: 'Ye- es, it must be so.'

'Very well. Do not imagine that I have not gone all emotional just because I happen to be in a female body, as many men like to suppose. To me, those goats represent myself in another form, for I identify Self as the only Reality, the Divine All. Man calls things by names, he divides, labels, analyses, scrutinizes, them - reaches conclusions. Nevertheless, the Divine is ALL. The Divine cannot be relegated to residing in man's soul alone, for if one believes this, then one does not worship an Omnipresent Deity. This is crystal clear. God must be the All, otherwise God is not a Supreme Being. Animals are none other than Sacred Life forms.'

By now, the Manager was pacing up and down the room, brow furrowed, lips compressed: 'They are likenesses, reflections of the Divine, as indeed we are...'

'The True Reality mirrors Itself, is that what you are saying?'

'In a sense, yes.'

'Then, everything created is Sacred. The Mirror reflects the Whole, not only a part. These concepts are given different terms, according to the viewpoint. For instance, the Metaphysician speaks of Spirit and Body – the Theologian, of the Word and the Flesh – the Biologist, names it, Life and Death – the Chemist, sees the Volatile and the Fixed, whilst the Physicist, understand it, to be High, Low, Fluidity and Density. One can go on. There is the Beautiful and the Ugly, Good and Evil.'

The Manager stood very still.

I made a move to leave, suddenly conscious of an inner weariness which swept over me like gathering thunder-clouds storming the sky. The shadow of my personal crisis hid my inner Rainbow, for try as I may, I had failed to hear even the echo of the cascades of laughter within my heart, for quite some time now, I had been close companion to sorrow. What was I doing here in this chair, talking to a stranger about the Inner life?

I was tired, weary beyond the telling. A hand touched my arm: 'Please, let my driver take you back to your Hotel,' the Manager said. I gratefully accepted his offer, thanking him for his courtesy and his concern. It was with relief that I slid into the passenger-seat.

The next day, the Manager telephoned, asking me to come to tea. He wished me to meet his Assistant, a younger man.

Life produces such surprises!

I had not been able to save two goats from suffering, but they had led me to help two humans adjust their inner compasses, which were not functioning very well. We had many talks. Hearts unburdened themselves, suggestions were put forward, and as is the way with miracles, the WAY became very luminous once more, made possible by Grace.

Before leaving that quiet, sleepy town, I walked one afternoon along a peaceful path close to a Churchyard, admiring the beautiful Birch trees towering above me. Sorrow draped my heart. I knew I could not escape from the reality of my personal problem. The surgical knife would have to be used. Suddenly, something made me stand still.

Before me was a barrel filled with water, and there, struggling in the centre of this barrel, was a large fly.

As had happened when I had seen the goats, everything appeared to recede into the background. My attention was centred wholly on that tiny creature battling so hard to survive. I put my hands into the water. It was ice-cold. The fly had ceased struggling.

Quickly, I picked it up, holding it in the palm of my hand. I leaned over the tiny body, breathed my warm breath over it, then cupped it with my other hand, and began walking with fast pace towards my hotel.

Every few seconds I would breathe on my motionless 'patient', cover it again with my hand, then hurry on.

I reached the Hotel in record time, rushed into my room, and carried on with my resuscitation efforts.

Seated beside the window, I looked down at the fly lying so still in my hand. I urged it on.

'Live, little on, live!' I told it, speaking from my heart.

Suddenly, I felt it stir. My heart leapt.

One fragile leg stretched out. Blessed movement!

Very gently, I placed the fly on the window-sill where, with infinite delicacy, it did its toilette.

Mesmerised, I watched the miracle of life.

Somehow, in that tiny frame, was my very Self. We were, both of us, representative of the mystery of suffering, which touches every created thing, as it dances the rhythm of life and apparent death.

Courage, hope, endurance, these, were the fires which must never be allowed to go out, and, even as I mused on this, a brilliant sunset touched the sky with vivid flames of glory.

I opened the window and watched as the fly spread his radiant wings to greet the coming night.

The brave creature had struggled so fiercely to live. There appeared to be no reason for hope, trapped in that water of ice, and yet, I had been brought to the spot.

I hope never to forget the wonderful lesson that fly taught me that solemn winter's day.

The well-known writer - Philosopher, Paul Brunton, displays his delicacy and sensitivity of spirit when he pens these words: 'Just before dusk every evening, and with the oncoming end of the violet sunset, a whistling thrush appears upon the stony patch which does duty for a stage for my bird companions and treats me to an excellent performance...strangest of all my comrades is a tame house-fly. Its favourite roost is on one of my thumb-nails. There it is content to pass its happy half hours in playful exploration. At suitable intervals I place some sugar in my hand and the fly clings to the food, no matter how I twist and turn my hand when writing, When I tire of supporting it on my thumbnail I transfer it to the other hand, where it remains perfectly contented.' We read further on: '...the humanity of that time lived by the light of a divine instinct and did not need to dally with the hesitations of cunning and intellect in order to understand what were its best interests...the animals of that age did not fear man and had no reason to fear him.'   3

Perhaps humanity will rediscover that Golden Age again.

* * *

The Right Word At The Right Time

It was a still, summer's night, the air redolent with the perfume of hidden flowers. Stars glowed brightly in their sky-palace, mysterious gems of light, which touched the soul with a harmony long-forgotten by the conscious self, yet still remembered by the wise unconscious.

I loved the stillness, the quiet hours which came after the day's activity. Drinking deep of the silence, I recharged my spiritual batteries, mulling over the book I had been reading by R. A. Schwaller de Lubicz, the savant-esotericist, who explained so superbly step by step, to the initiate, the hidden teachings of the Inner Temple, once accessible to seekers of Truth in centres situated in Egypt, Greece, and in other parts of the ancient world.

Something cold touched my sandaled feet. A slug was making its way across it. I leaned down, picked it up, walked towards the flower-beds and laid the small creature amongst the nasturtiums.

I went for my torch, shone it on the ground, searching for other slugs.

'What are you doing?'

My neighbour looked over the fence at me. She was a very pleasant woman.

'I am saving these slugs and snails from being crushed by our feet,' was my reply.

'Do you do this every night?'

'Yes.'

My friend laughed: 'Why bother, Gladys, when you go to the Butcher's shop and buy meat from him? Are you not being rather a hypocrite?'

We conversed for a while longer, then, I went inside to think.

Katie was right. I never killed anything deliberately. Every insect found, was tenderly attended to, yet, I ate flesh. I was indeed a hypocrite!

In the 'Imitation of Christ', its author, Thomas â Kempis writes that every word uttered is ordained by God.

This is precisely what had happened this night. Katie my neighbour, had said the right words at the right time, when my heart was ready to receive them with understanding, able to face their truth squarely, without attempting to justify myself, or make excuses.

I resolved to become a vegetarian from that moment on.

My family were thrown off balance by my decision, voicing their concerns in no uncertain manner.

Knowing I had been studying World Religions for many years, my father, who was an ardent Catholic (like myself), was ever his forthright self: 'It comes from reading all about Buddhism and Hinduism. You are being influenced by all this, that is what has happened. Catholicism does not teach we should become vegetarians, so why should you become one? Tell us truthfully, are you intending to follow another religion?'

'Papa, why on earth should I change my religion? I am studying other Religions in order to better understand my own. The Heart of all religions is the same…there is only One Unique Divine Source.'

'Well, let us not get into that, now. As long as you do not get carried away by all this esotericism, I am the first to believe your motives are sincere. If this is what you want to do, then, so be it.'

Maman's loving gaze enfolded me as warmly as her arms: 'As long as your health does not suffer, my bien aimée.' As long as you do not get carried away by all this esotericism, I am the first to believe your motives are sincere. If this is what you want to do, then, I am all for it. I know you will not stray from your principles, but I will ask Doctor Shedrow, if you will require supplementary vitamins, just in case.'

So it was, that because of a slug, a neighbour's true assessment of the situation, I became a vegetarian.

In doing so, I opened the door to much ridicule, and often to open hostility in some cases.

One such occasion was at the launching of one of my children's books. Mr Marais, my Afrikaans publisher, introduced me to a novelist. As he moved away, the woman eyed me with open distaste: 'So, I hear that you are one of THEM!'

I waited.

She waved her glass in languid gesture. 'You know! I mean, you are a vegetarian! One of those who are always rabbiting on to us about being cannibals and so on. Such arrogance I think! Of course, Sarel tells me you are writing a book on World Religions, and this story of yours which is just published, is a Fairytale. Typical! You will never make the Bestseller List that way, you know. You must be one of those altruistic types……well, let me tell you that the public want meat in their reading – lusty, gusty stuff. And, that is just what I give them.'

I made no comment, noting the feverish glitter in her eyes. She was a restless spirit.

As though irritated by my lack of response, she sipped quickly the champagne she had been given: 'Why did you not have your Fairytale published in English? That is your mother-tongue.'

I smiled at her: 'I tried, but the publishers said it was too original a story.'

She pounced on that: 'There, what did I tell you! A vegetarian is a show-off. Wants to prove how different he or she is…you even have to be different in your writing.'

My smile was there again: 'Well, Sarel Marais did not reject it. Here is Sugarbush, in black and white. I am very proud of my Fairytale, and you are quite right, I dare to be myself. If that is being different, then, I stand accused. I will not apologize for being me. And now, what of you? What books have you written?'

Gradually, the hostility towards me receded, as the young woman spoke animatedly about her work.

I would encounter attitudes like hers, many times. In fact, when my book 'Your God Is My God', was published, a man raced down the stairs of my home, screaming: 'Blasphemy! Blasphemy!', because I had told him that for me, God is present everywhere – yes, even in animals.

Strange reaction from a man who had converted to different religions many times, and had come to me, with what he had called 'an open mind.'

One day, out of the blue, I was taken to Hospital to undergo surgery.

When I returned home, Rusty licked my hand lying outside the coverlet; Snappy stared at me with his lovely brown eyes, worried and glad at the same time, his cream-coloured tail beating the air in its own mysterious dance.

Miko settled on my left, Nou-Nou, on my right, whilst Sita and Li - Li draped themselves across my feet.

I told them that I loved them, then, we fell asleep, except for Rusty and Snappy, who took their roles as sentinels, very seriously, positioning themselves like two lions in front of my door.

Nou- Nou did not approve of me whistling. Whenever she heard me whistle, she would gently lay her paw across my lips, regarding me the while with solemn look: 'Ladies do not whistle,' she seemed to be telling me.

Whenever I was sad, Nou-Nou would come to me, her soul-antennae having detected the tears within my heart. She knew me unerringly.

With ever so delicate a touch, she would give me her special kiss, taking my cheek in her mouth, and gently holding it for a few seconds, then, she would seat herself on my desk and stare into my eyes with a look which conveyed so much: 'I am here. I understand. I love you. Be brave. Endure. You are not alone. Remember that. You are surrounded by those who love you.'

I would often look at these mysteries Man calls 'animals', and wonder at them. Each individual was unique, occupying a space-volume called 'form', which vibrated with such intense 'mystique.' How could one possibly hope to classify such intangibles, which impacted so strongly on one's soul?

Their presence soothed, healed, uplifted, amused, entranced.

One day, Rusty followed Guillaume out of the gates, only to receive a brick full in the face, thrown by a drunk African.

I rushed over to Dr Davis's surgery. Rusty's blood had spattered over me. Although very sore, the Doberman had allowed me to handle him.

Another time, my black –and- tan-friend rushed into my room, shaking his head vigorously. He had been in a fight. One ear flopped at an eerie angle, crimson blotches appeared on my walls, as the shaking continued.

Placing a towel round his head, I affixed it with some large safety pins, drove Rusty to the Vet's once again. Stitches, and injection, then, back home, where the Doberman convalesced in style.

Next, it was Snappy's turn. He hurt his back as he leaped into the air to catch a ball. He yelped with pain, then lay in a heap on the ground, brown eyes pleading for help.

I drove along the familiar road to the Animal Clinic, then, brought my patient back home to a relieved pet colony.

When I worked with my mother at her Hotel in Berea, I took charge of the Linen room as one of my duties. A cheery Cockney lady was our Housekeeper. We get along famously.

One morning, on a visit to my African ladies in the Laundry Rooms, I caught sight of two small kittens. One glimpse, then, they vanished.

I got down on hands and knees, searching for them.

'Aie! Miss Gladys, you are getting all dirty,' Margaret the Laundry Maid called out, looking over her fleshy shoulder as she ironed.

Margaret was one of my favourites. She had told me when I asked her why she was always eating: 'I am figureless for a long time now, but men find me very beautiful. We, Africans, are a nice size – not like you, Miss Gladys, you are a broom!'

Everyone had laughed heartily at these words, and Margaret had been delighted by this reaction.

'I will give a Bonsela (reward), to anyone who brings me these kittens,' I declared, as I dusted my knees, and moved away.

Very soon, there was a beaming face at my office door. It was Margaret, holding out two tiny morsels of fur, enormous violet eyes dominating the lovely faces.

I took 'Tickey' and 'Sixpence' from her, placed them on a pillow, opened my purse to fish out the Bonsela. Margaret grinned, took the money, and returned to the Laundry.

'Cor! I don't think I will like them kittens,' said the Housekeeper, eyeing the new arrivals, 'I have never had any.'

'They are so tiny,' I said, 'they must be starving. I will get some milk for them. Just keep an eye on them, Mrs Metcalfe, please.'

'Well, all right then,' she agreed, good soul that she was.

I came back with a saucer filled with warm milk.

Two pink tongues went to work, huge eyes surveyed us curiously when the saucer was empty.

I organized a warm, fluffy place for them, hidden from view. I did not want anyone to know of my 'find', just yet.

Mrs Metcalfe proved to be a stout ally, and, in time, she grew to tolerate our stowaways, watching as I smuggled in, sardines mixed with rice, etc.,

Weeks passed. Tickey and Sixpence were now old enough to face the outside world. I brought them into the Office, placed them before maman: 'This is Tickey, and this is Sixpence,' I told her.

'I know,' my incredible maman told me, 'I saw them when they were very small, but I decided to let you tell me in your own time." She twinkled at me: 'I also know you have been feeding wild cats ever since you came here. When I asked Fickson (the head Chef), where the food remains were going to, he said he was keeping them for Miss Gladys's 'bebies."

We both burst out laughing, then, we hugged.

It was true. I had asked Fickson to put all the food which was not being used, in a tray specially reserved for me. Every day, I put this food into old dishes I had placed outside near the perimeter of the property. Many wild cats were fed in this way. I also saw to it there was plenty of fresh water for them.

Lakshmi arrived on the premises one day. She looked like a squirrel, with her long, silky black hair. Her eyes were a striking blue. Refined, delicate in her manners, she walked unafraid amongst our guests, settling in the sun like a lizard, with her tail curled around her body like a question mark.

She was very friendly with Tickey and Sixpence, watching them with the benign look of aristocracy on frolicking peasants.

One day, she disappeared.

We suspected a guest had spirited her away.

I missed her regal presence about the place, her aura of serenity. Her favourite seats were now empty of her grace and beauty. The Jacaranda tree at the entrance of the Hotel, mourned.

One year later, Lakshmi came into the office, scratched at the bottom drawer until we opened it, then she gave birth to kittens. They did not survive, so, I took Lakshmi home, where she could relax, for there was a haunted look in her eyes, which told of unhappy times; perhaps her kidnapping had scarred her. We tried to give her back her sense of security, and I think we succeeded in part, for she was mantled once again in noble grace, walking alongside Nou-Nou, no doubt telling the matriarch about her experiences after the abduction, of her escape, her trek back to the Hotel, the loss of her litter.

A speeding car ended Lakshmi's earth-life. I see her draped in serene loveliness, watching us with her lapis -lazuli eyes, from a shining Star in Heaven.

■■■

Snappy had been with us seven years, when he fell ill.

Doctor Davis told me that it was serious. I held Snappy's creamy beauty to me, even as I sought reassurance that he would get better. None was forthcoming.

An icy finger of dread clutched at my heart. The pain of it!

I looked deep into those eyes, whose loving gaze had been like a second skin, ever shadowing me, tender, true, warm like hearth-flames, when the heart-soul shivers.

It was unbearable sorrow, and yet, it had to be borne.

Snappy died the next day.

I was heartbroken. Everyone commiserated, but the ice in my heart would not thaw.

We buried the treasure known to us as Snappy, beneath the Oak tree whose friendly presence Snappy had so often sought.

Tatti had prepared a Headstone for the occasion. Papa gave me some of his special roses to place on the newly-dug grave. Nou-Nou and the other members of the Cat family, attended, as did splendid Rusty, standing stiff and alert, intelligent eyes fixed on us.

I was inconsolable.

Next, it was Rusty. He waited for my son to come home, before suddenly collapsing in his arms. His heart stopped even as Guillaume cradled him.

He too, was buried in our garden.

From the flat rooftop of our home, I would gaze out at the places where the two, Snappy and Rusty, had paced together, ran happily about together, had rested together.

I had been blessed to have shared their soul-beauty for awhile, now, I had to enter my 'secret Heart-closet' to commune with them.

Miko was found dead one morning. My beautiful, heroic warrior, had also left this world. He too, sat beside Lakshmi, Snappy and Rusty in the heavenly skies of Love!

Li - Li and Sita did not return home one day.

Before their disappearance, Nou-Nou came to me, dragging one paw on the ground. She lay at my feet, gave a cry of pain, then tried to lick her hurt front pay, moaning.

Doctor Davis to the rescue. He told me: 'Looks like someone threw a large stone at her. Her leg is broken. I will have to put it into plaster.'

Once back home, Nou-Nou hopped about on three legs, whilst my pet Colony gathered round her to stare at her strange-looking appendage, swathed in a wall of hardness. They sniffed at it with twitching noses, eyes round with wonder, tails waving and curling as though sending out coded messages, senses on the alert, sharpened by the strong odour of 'that place', where sharp objects pierced your flesh, strange long sleeps swept over you, suddenly. Their unease was so apparent that I treated them all to their favourite snack; 'La Vache Qui Rit' creamy cheese, tucked away specially for them.

Nou-Nou settled in my lap for hours at a time, taking full advantage of the situation, unashamedly demanding long conversations in our secret language.

Then, this remarkable cat-person proved once again, just how wise she was! On the day the plaster cast was to be taken off her leg, she stepped out of it, leaving some hairs stuck to the inside. Doctor Davis was delighted with her. I kept the plaster cast for years.

But now, her life-cycle on this earth was drawing to a close.

This time, she was struck a cruel blow on her back.

I wept as I held her in my arms. The doctor tried to take her paw, but she withdrew it gently. She placed it in my palm, her wonderful eyes never leaving my face. As the injection entered her body, she died, still gazing at me with love.

She took with her a very precious part of my heart. I gave it willingly, for Nou-Nou was the Mother in the form of Cat-hood. When she withdrew into her essence, I wept tears of crystal, for these tears came from pure depths, a reverent well, a Sacred spring! Nou-Nou still wears these diamonds about her lovely head, a Tiara of love in her celestial home.

The day of Nou-Nou's death I wrote a poem to her:

Nou-Nou

———

Nou-Nou whose name originates in the timeless womb of Life,
You came to me courageous and bleeding, thirsty, hungry,
Exhausted, in the physical casement named Cat-hood.
Yet within you has ever been, and ever will be, for me,
A moral fibre, a spiritual beauty, an undaunted spirit
Which, like a benediction, has laid its seal upon my heart.

A beauty beyond description, you carry within you.
Gentle, loving, wonderful manifestation of the Mother.
Your paw comforted me on my face, your eyes caressed me
When I was sad.
Your mouth kissed me when your love wished to
Express itself.
In your eyes shone a light which irradiated the darkest
Depths of my soul.
Before what you are in Truth, I am mute.

Now, your presence is denied me in the physical, but
Your glory is mine as heaven-sent Gift, for all eternity.
Thank you, O my God for having given me a guide,
Mentor, companion, so faithful and lovely.

Nou-Nou, what can ever separate this Power of Love?
We are together always. I love you.
Thank you for loving me.

———

My sister brought me a beautiful puppy, a red-gold wonder, whom we called Rajah. My son, in particular, loved him deeply. I was still too scarred by recent animal-bereavements to respond as I would have wished to this lovely Dog-person. When my son went overseas to study, Rajah missed him terribly. He fell ill, and Doctor Davis told me he was dying. A merciful injection released Rajah from this earth-life. My son felt Rajah's death, deeply. The one consolation was to know that the beautiful pet had not suffered.

■■■

When I worked in London, I bought seeds for some pigeons, when the harshness of winter arrived.

To my astonishment, workers from a nearby building, complained to my Boss about my feeding 'vermin.'

'This is my window-sill,' I told him, 'I refuse to be bullied by these people. It is my money, my office. I will continue feeding these birds.'

And that was that!

Next, it was my neighbour downstairs, who put in a complaint to my landlord. Apologetically, he paid me a visit. I looked at him sternly: 'Is this my flat? Do I not pay you the rent you ask, for this space?'

'You do. Yes, it is your flat,' he agreed.

Steel entered my voice: 'When you visit Venice, do you not rush to San Marco's Square to feed the pigeons, or take photographs or people doing so?'

He looked down.

'Yet, because we are in London, we should allow these birds to starve in winter? Is that consistent behaviour? Another thing, I do not interfere with my neighbour playing that loud cacophony he calls music, until the early hours of the morning, which prevents us from enjoying our well-earned rest. He must not interfere with my wish to keep a few birds from starving. This is a democracy after all, or am I being naïve?'

I heard no more from that particular neighbour, and my birds continued to receive their little bit of food.

When living in Wimbledon, I was incensed one Sunday afternoon, when I heard gunfire coming from my neighbour's garden. Shortly after, a pigeon fell on my lawn, mortally wounded. I immediately called the police out to investigate shooting in a residential area. The Law quickly stopped the murderer next door from what the man called his 'sport'.

Animal-lovers are warriors of the heart. They must stand up for their vulnerable friends, not shrink and cower from the bullies of this world. There is absolutely no excuse for cruelty. I campaigned vigorously when rabbits were being cruelly slaughtered, and also against certain abattoirs, whose treatment of cattle was barbaric. Regarding the latter, I submitted photographs taken by my late cousin, Roger Bax de Keating, to the appropriate authorities, and they assured me that steps would be taken to put a stop to such practices that he had tried so hard to have abolished.

■■

'Man is called a rational animal, because he is endowed with mind and capable of acquiring knowledge. Other animals – those on the ground and in the air who possess voice - breathe and have a soul. All things that grow and decrease can be called alive because they live and grow, but it cannot be said that all such things have soul. There are four kinds of living beings: - some of them are immortal and have souls, such as angels, others have mind, soul and breath, such as men, yet others have soul and breath, such as animals.'

(St. Antony the Great, from "The Philokalia)

Mauritius, that dreamy isle, embraces many races and cultures in benign arms. The Hindu, Muslim, Buddhist, Christian, Taoist or Shintoist, all live in peace, harmoniously accommodating one another, tolerant and non-aggressive in their attitudes to one another's customs. Fundamentalism has no place here, with the result that the populace is relaxed, smiling, friendly, easy-going, as though in perpetual holiday-mood.

The delicate minarets of a Mosque gleam in the brilliant sunlight as the Call to Prayer floats on the air. Shiva and his consort, Parvarti, grace a Hindu Temple, fragrant flowers adorning their statues; the ruby lamp glows in the Catholic Church where candles are lit before the Madonna and her Christ-Babe, illuminating their gentle expressions. Beside a Taoist Monastery, sparkling fountains sound their music of peace in tranquil grounds, here, there is a serenity conducive to meditation; at another shrine, pilgrims pay homage to Buddha, placing tapers before the harmonious statues of the Blessed One.

The land itself is of volcanic origin, and the terrain rises to a plateau that covers the central part of the island where several lakes are located. From the highlands, clear streams flow in sparkling loveliness to the coast. The beaches are superb, with fine, golden sands stretching for miles, caressed by turquoise water so transparent that one can see the spiked urchins nestling on the ocean bed. A magnificent coral reef almost encircles the entire tropical paradise.

It was also the home of the Dodo, a stout, flightless bird, of the Raphus Cucullatus family, whose size was that of a large turkey. It possessed a heavy hooked bill, and blue- grey plumage, complete with short, fluffy feathers at the tail. The islands of nearby Rodriguez and Reunion, were also hosts to the Dodo, until the year 1681, when the bird became extinct.

Sugar-cane plantations occupy 90% of the Agricultural land, and there are also tea-plantations, and food crops, grown.

English is the official language, but 'créole', a French patois or dialect, is widely spoken.

My husband and I came to this island, leaving our respective jobs in London.

During our eight months on the island, we fostered many cats.

The first arrival was Mimou, a male of about six weeks old, who had been abandoned near our property on Christmas Eve. Terrified, hungry and thirsty, he poured forth his litany of protests into the night.

I gathered up the small creature from the stony ground, and brought him into the bungalow set far back from the road, a graceful palm tree rising from the front patio, tall fronds making musical sounds in the sea-breeze.

Eyes filled with wonderment stared into my face, even as the mouth continued uttering sounds of distress, the small paws clinging to me in desperation.

Soon, a saucer of milk evoked strong purring, as the waif dipped his tongue delicately to quench a mighty thirst.

Mimou slept on my pillow that first night, but from the next day which was Christmas, and saw my husband's arrival on the Island, he curled up against a male head, which was only right, seeing he had been presented to my spouse as one of his Christmas presents.

He was a delightful 'toy' from the very start, running along after us as fast as his little legs could carry him, eyes glowing with vivid 'joie de vivre', despite the ordeal of abandonment.

One morning I called my husband to witness the astonishing sight of Mimou perched over the shower drain, a solemn look of ecstasy on his face as he passed water.

We laughed behind our hands, so as not to offend the small person so intent upon stepping into the 'place of cleaning' where he had watched us wash ourselves, and was now performing a rite of his own.

From that moment, Mimou was furnished with his very own mobile toilet, a bright orange plastic tub, filled with gravel. It became his special favourite possession, a 'thing' he visited even when he had no need to, simply because it was his very own.

My husband used to call Mimou whenever the bright object had received its clean gravel, and, like a bullet, the grey and black bundle of fur, would come streaking across the parquet flooring, skidding and sliding as he came, eyes shining with happiness. Once the 'toy' had been put in its place, Mimou would inspect it scrupulously, tail held high like a salute.

He was a constant source of amusement.

His enthusiasm sent him flying on the rugs we had spread on the floors, an amazed look on his face as he was propelled whither he knew not. Other times, he would rush under furniture to escape the Polisher, which, no doubt, had the look of a monster to the kitten.

He was quite unique in the way he copied the poses my husband adopted when he slept.

We would see him lie on his back on the sofa, then bend his two front paws over his chest as he had seen his human father do. Later, he would stretch out his back legs, and keep them still.

Every night, he would come over to my side to purr against my cheek as I read, but when I had switched off the light, he would cross over our pillows to nestle against my husband's hair. A loud purring would tell us that he was about to put his cat lights out for the night, then, quiet would descend. Mimou, like his protector, was asleep, leaving me to experience envy at such an ability to switch off instantly.

One of the colourful characters we met on the Island, was a fisherman-cum-gardener, whose name was Tiban. He had worked for years on my cousin's property, and often took us sailing in the lagoon.

Tiban was a Créole, with a small, muscular body and a happy, friendly expression on his good-looking face. He had very expressive yes in which danced twinkling lights. They were indicative of his innate sense of fun. He laughed often.

He did odd jobs for us, remaining afterwards, to sample cold beer, a treat he really enjoyed. Whilst he relaxed, he regaled us with stories to which we were only too eager to lend captive ear.

This day, he embarked with enthusiasm on his tale, which was interspersed with flashes of white teeth as his grin appeared at regular intervals; 'Well, you must know that there are many strange people in the world. one day, I am in my boat, you know the one I mean, it is the boat belonging to the boss, and he comes up to me and says; 'Tiban, we are having a lady coming over later, and she is staying the night here. I want you to help her with her suitcases and so forth. Tend to her needs. She will be next door at six o'clock. You must bring her here." I say; "Yes, M'sieu", and I go on with my work. At six o'clock sharp, I walk to the house where there are people singing very loudly. There they are, holding candles and raising them high in the air. I think to myself, why are they needing candles? There is a lot of light everywhere. Still, who can tell why people do foolish things. I wait under the palm tree until all this noisy singing is over, then, I wait some more, because they are all screaming: "Hallelujah! Hallelujah! New Jerusalem!"'

Here, Tiban slaps his thigh, his face alight with laughter.

We join in, vizualizing the scene.

Tiban resumes: 'Now, they hand over the candles to a man in a long white gown. He does not smile, but keeps on saying: "Bless you," as the people pass. I think to myself he can't be a priest because his gown is different, but, who knows what he was? Everybody treated him like children do at school. Now, a lady is seen, carrying a suitcase. I go forward, and take it from her. We come to the house, I show her to the room. She tells me to put the suitcase on the bed. I think I can go now, so, I move away.

The lady says: "Do not go. Stay here, and see the power of the Lord." Well, I obey, and I stand still. To tell you the truth, I was not feeling too good about this lady being in the house, because I had overheard my boss saying to Madame his wife, that he did not want a person belonging to a sect, camping in his house, which is a good Catholic home. When this lady, who had also been holding a candle high in the air, told me that she would show me the power of the Lord, I wanted to leave that room at once. Still, my boss had told me to see to her, so I stayed where I was – near to the door. Now, this lady suddenly hits the suitcase hard with her hand, saying: "Open, open, in the Name of Jesus!" Of course, the suitcase did not move! I felt so sorry for this lady, so I said to her: "Let me try to open it." Her face was very red, her eyes were big, round like an alarm clock…then, I pressed the catch, and voila! The suitcase opened.'

By this time, we were convulsed with laughter. Tears spurted from Tiban's eyes. When he was calm enough, he resumed: 'Such foolishness! We all know that when you want to start a car, you must use the key, then turn it, so that the engine will start – Jesus gives us the brains to know this – but Jesus tells us to help ourselves. You cannot expect the Lord to come and do everything for us – so, why did God give us arms, legs, and a brain for? Oh, that poor lady, telling Jesus to open a simple suitcase for her. When she left the house the next day, I threw some holy water over the floor of her bedroom. Such foolishness can remain on walls and furniture, you know.'

When Tiban left us, we were still laughing.

Our loud laughter had somewhat unsettled Mimou, who had beat a hasty retreat under my knitting.

Mauritius was once called l'Ile de France. Many of my ancestors fled the French Revolution to seek asylum on this beautiful island, so far from the Motherland.

These aristocrats settled on large estates where sugar-cane was grown, for the most part. Their lives pursued their course in comfortable elegance, with slaves ever ready to respond to a clap of the hands.

One of my favourite heroines of those dark times in the history of France, when Terror stalked the land, was Madame Roland, who had written: 'Today on a throne, to-morrow in a prison. Such is the fate of virtue in revolutionary times. Enlightened men, who have pointed out its rights are, by a nation weary of oppression, first called into authority. But it is not possible that they should maintain their places. The ambitious, eager to take advantage of circumstances, mislead the people by flattery, and to acquire consequence and power, prejudice themselves against their real friends. Men of principle, who despise adulation, and contemn intrigue, meet not their oppressors on equal terms; their fall is therefore certain; the still soft voice of sober reason, amidst the tumult of the passions, is easily overpowered.'

Arrested by the myrmidons of the Revolutionary Committee, Madame Roland was first taken to the Abbaye, then, transferred to the prison of St. Pelagie, where she remained five months in confinement.

She displayed great fortitude during all that time, remarking: 'If t his is the reward of virtue on earth, who can be astonished at my contempt of life, or at the resolution with which I look death in the face.'

Madame Roland showed heroic firmness on the scaffold, as her hair was cut off, her hands bound. Before placing her head on the block, she bowed to the statue of Liberty, then, uttered words full of pathos: 'Oh, Liberty! What crimes are committed in thy name!'

We had left London, intending to settle in Mauritius with my mother, who had been a widow now, for two years, but this was not to be. Maman was suddenly hospitalised. I immediately flew across to Johannesburg, where my sister Jacqueline, and my brother Francis, met me at the Airport. From there we drove straight to our maman's bedside. A week later, maman died in our arms, at my sister's home. We were inconsolable.

Back in Mauritius, my husband battened down doors and windows, as a cyclone hit the island, throwing trees about, like straws, hurling roofs through the air, whining, wailing, moaning, howling, in dreadful cacophony of sound, whilst humans and animals cowered from the raging fury of nature.

Mimou was petrified. He clung to his human father with four trembling paws, eyes dilated with terror, mouth open in screams of pure anguish. To calm him, Vincent placed Mimou's small, quivering frame inside his shirt, holding him there, with one hand.

I heard about the cyclone, on Television, as telephone poles were down, and there was no means of communication possible. I could only hope and pray that Vincent and Mimou were out of harm's way, whilst I tried to deal with the cyclone which raged pitilessly within my heart, following my beloved maman's death.

When I returned to the island two weeks later, the ravages left in the cyclone's wake, were sharply apparent. Roads had to be negotiated with care, as there were still subsidences occurring, and rock-falls to be expected.

Mimou had grown. He had recovered his composure, skipping along after his mobile toilet held in father's hands, avidly demolishing food and drink placed in his dish on a plastic mat in the kitchen, playing the role of socks to our ankles, as we walked about the property, as he was very nervous of large dogs passing by the fence, barking as they went. Once they were out of sight, Mimou would walk confidently beside us, eyes everywhere – just in case, he made sure that he had trouser and leg-cover for shelter.

One day, I caught the flicker of a tail – there it was again! I stood still. A beautiful face appeared, the rest of the body followed.

She was a Cat-lady, pure-white, with small tan and dark-grey patches on her hindquarters. Her eyes were oriental, almond-shaped, of a brilliant, sparkling green.

Her name sprang from my heart.

This is Mamushka! The Mother.

We looked at one another for a while.

She accepted my heart's offering, with natural grace, as though being paid homage to, was an everyday occurrence.

I placed food and drink for her, at some distance from the patio.

She must have been very hungry and thirsty, but she remained where she was whilst she scented the air, her eyes scanning every piece of the property with a precision born from hard-earned experience, then, she walked at leisurely pace towards the feast awaiting her beneath the banana trees.

Her alertness was her shield, even as she devoured the food, her tail never ceasing its twitching. She closed her eyes in ecstasy when she drank the milk and the cream.

Once again, she levelled her gaze at me, then, she was gone, hidden by the thick undergrowth adjoining the property.

I hoped she would be back.

Mamushka came twice a day, remaining always at the same spot, wrapping her tail about her as casually as women do, with their stoles. She was a marvel of grace, holding one paw in the air as she interrupted her toilette to turn inwards on a dream........she would remain in that pose for seconds, caught in an inner reverie which captivated her, then, slowly, she would continue with her toilette, pink tongue tirelessly licking the splendid fur.

Mimou watched her, fascinated, yet too scared to venture close. Mamushka flicked one glance in his direction, then turned her attention elsewhere.

As the weeks passed, it became apparent that Mamushka was pregnant.

She did not appear for a few days. I grew concerned for her safety, as we were told that another cyclone was on its way.

Tiban reassured us as he cut down coconuts from the tree in our back garden: 'This time, it is the child of the Big Wind, which is coming – yes, there will be damage, but not too much! Better to get the bananas in too, I will cut them, so, and so.'

His machete flashed, down came the bananas. I took some fruit and offered them to our friendly worker. Vincent gave him a glass of beer.

Tiban drank thirstily, took a cigarette proffered by his host.

Screwing up his eyes as though to focus his thoughts, Tiban said: 'The tourists are going around carrying their cameras, waiting to take snaps of the cyclone.' He burst out laughing, slapped his thigh, forgetting his cigarette which shot through the air. He quickly retrieved it, dusted it off, then, shook his head: 'How can they think of photos, when the world is roaring like a made Loup Garou (werewolf), about them? These tourists! You can see they know nothing about cyclones. When we had our big one, in December last year, I saw a red-haired man taking a walk a few minutes before we were hit. I took his arm, rushed him inside a house, and left him there. I don't know what language he was using, but I had not time to talk. Tourists!'

His delightful laugh pealed out; 'You know, I will tell you this story. It is about Gadiadhar. Some years ago, the police were looking all over the place for this bandit. Heaven knows what mischief he had been up to – how many people he had killed. He used to hide in the cane fields, then spring on his victim, slit his throat, then, take his money.'

Tiban looked at us to see what effect this alarming tale had produced. Satisfied, he continued, dropping his voice somewhat: 'Now, everyone was nervous. Gadiadhar this, Gadiadhar that! A door slammed, and people cried out: "Gadiadhar!" I tell you, panic swept the land. The police could not find him. Is that so strange? When do police find anyone? Anyhow, this day, and

Indian businessman was walking along a road thinking his thoughts, as we all do, for it would be crazy to think someone else's thoughts for them.'

We laughed at his droll humour.

Merry lights danced in the storyteller's eyes: 'Now then, we have this Indian returning home from work. There he was, the good fellow, minding his own business, walking near the bright- green cane fields, when, of a sudden, an apparition appeared beside him. It was a tall figure draped in the most awful black. From head to toe it was veiled – it appeared to float.......even as the man stared, this phantom uttered a terrible shriek. Filled with horror, overcome by a sudden faintness, the man closed his eyes, silently praying to Lord Krishna to save him from this demon. When he opened his eyes again, the creature had vanished.'

Tiban drew on the stub of his cigarette, finished his beer, regarded us with scarcely-contained excitement: 'This is a true story I am telling – be sure it is.'

'What happened next?' I asked.

'I will say. Now, this apparition was none other than a widow. She was coming from Church, when all of a sudden she saw this Indian at her side – you see, he had come out of the short- cut through the cane fields, and she screamed with terror, because she thought he was the bandit Gadiadhar. She rushed into the first house she saw, where she told the occupants that she had just met the villain the police were searching for. At that moment the doorbell rang again. On the threshold stood the Indian businessman, eyes starting from his head: "Madame," he told the lady of the house, "may I stay here awhile. I have just met a phantom on the road…" The woman ushered him in while he was still busy explaining. The widow caught sight of him: "Gadiadhar! He is here!" The Indian shouted: "Rama, save me! It is the demon." What a commotion. Servants came running, armed with pots and pans, having heard the name 'Gadiadhar.' The widow was given smelling salts… what a thing! You see, it was the woman who was wearing her widow- weeds, who had nearly given the poor man a heart-attack. These long, black skirts, and the face completely veiled…I never like to look on such a person, myself, I can tell you.'

Tiban slapped his thigh, tears glistened in his eyes.

We never tired of hearing his tales.

The second cyclone struck. This time, as Tiban had predicted, it was a milder one. Nevertheless, it was scary, with the sky turning an ominous colour, forecast of the eerie silence which settled before the wind struck the Island with sudden fury, howling like a host of banshees set loose upon us.

I hap put Mimou into a knitted cap which I hung across my neck. He stayed there, huge eyes fixed on my face, whilst the cyclone raged about us. I soothed him by caressing him, talking to him, kissing him, giving him licks of cream on my fingers.

Where was Mamushka?

When the cyclone abated, Vincent and I, went about clearing the garden of debris, anxiously searching for the green-eyed Mamushka, but without success.

She surfaced the following day, carrying a tiny morsel in her mouth. She put it down behind the fallen bole of a tree, in our garden. She disappeared, to return, carrying a second kitten. Again, she placed it behind the trunk. Yet a third time, then, Mamushka settled with her kittens.

I was elated. The wild creature trusted us enough to bring her precious family on to the property.

Mimou was not allowed to approach. Mamushka sent him away with such spitting that he sped as though shot from a bow.

I placed food and milk near the tree-trunk, then, went away.

Vincent and I watched from our bedroom window.

Pointed ears like those of foxes, were the first to emerge, followed by round eyes filled with the wonder which makes young creatures so entrancing; tiny mouths a-quiver for food.

They quickly joined their mother when she gave them permission to partake of the dishes she had sampled. Like a lioness, she stood guard over them whilst they ate.

And with good reason. A dog wandered in one day, sniffing around as he smelled the odour of food. Mamushka launched herself through the air without a second's hesitation, landing on the dog's face. He jerked away, screaming. Mamushka raked her claws across his sensitive nose, causing him to arch his back, paws waving the air in frantic effort to escape, then he was gone, sounding his pain as he fled.

Mamushka stared after him, body rigid with tension and fury, then, she turned to look at her startled family satisfying herself that they were safe and sound. She sounded her special signal to them. Obediently, they disappeared from sight.

Her jewel-eyes raked the surroundings, tail flailing the air with whip-like motion, muscular body alert for the return of the enemy, but we never saw a dog again on the premises, because Vincent placed chicken-wire everywhere.

One day I spied a round tummy on sturdy legs. It went into the kitchen. I peeped in. It was one of Mamushka's children, grey and black in colour.

Vincent gave her the name 'Hollow - Legs', because she danced so lightly as she walked.

Mimou gaped at the intruder. What on earth was this?

Undeterred, the kitten waddled over to Mimou's food, sniffed it, but got no further. Her mother rushed in, gave her a sharp nip, ordering her back outside. Quick as a flash, the little one bolted.

Weeks passed, then, one balmy evening, as we sat on the patio with Mimou scouting around, Mamushka made a regal appearance, herding her three children before her, introducing them to us formally at last.

I waited for Mamushka to choose her spot before speaking to our visitors in special; 'we welcome you' tones.

The mother looked at us with her emerald yes, a long, searching approving look, then she lay down in relaxed posture, happy to let her kittens explore the patio and Mimou.

The latter sprang into my lap, alarmed at this invasion of his territory, eyes growing bigger as he observed the antics of the spirited trio. Apart from Hollow Legs, one was white with ginger blotches, whilst the other was black, so we called them Ginger and Blackie.

I decided to let them taste some 'Vache Qui Rit' cheese, which I placed in small pieces on the patio stone-work.

Mamushka sampled it, approved, sounded an 'all- clear' signal. Her kittens quickly ate up. Mimou approached his piece warily, but could not resist the delicious morsel.

Soon, he was gambolling about with the kittens, an expression of delight on his face, for he had acquired playmates at last.

Mamushka's trust in us deepened. One day, she did us the honour of stepping inside our living-room, herding her precious charges before her. Our rugs became transformed into flying carpets as Mimou joined in the wrestling and chasing, as four exuberant young cats made whoopee. Mamushka kept manners on her brood, charging at them to discipline them whenever necessary.

It was a delight to see also, how she played with them, pinning them down, then licking them with loving tongue.

When Mimou played truant, refusing to come into the house at bedtime, Mamushka gave away his hiding place, by seating herself under the tree where he had hidden. She knew, as we did, that he was too young to fight the powerful Toms who roamed about at night.

Our Cat Colony settled into a harmonious daily round, but Mamushka kept her young ones outside, sometimes disappearing with them for days at a time, taking them no doubt, on survival courses. Mimou waited for them wistfully. Mamushka never took him with her family until much later.

Mimou was our alarm clock, licking me early in the morning on behalf of the hungry brood eagerly awaiting me outside the kitchen door. Every evening, I prepared a dish of rice and sardines, knowing that the 'I am hungry – I am starving' cat-cries, would not cease until the mouths were busy wolfing down some food. Next, they received milk and dollops of cream. Water was also at hand for them outside, on the kitchen veranda. Elevenses consisted of diced bread in milk, in which I had mixed some honey. The one o'clock meal was served, then, on special days, ice-cream topped the bill, sending tails into quivers of ecstasy.

Meanwhile, Vincent and I visited the Island. At Quatre-Bornes, we strolled about the market, enjoying the sights and sounds. There were stalls piled high with purple aubergines, lush, ripe tomatoes, marrows, bright-green lettuce, endive, large carrots, peppers, chilies of all sizes, vegetables too numerous to mention…the fruit was mouth-watering. Paw-paws, litchis, mangoes, pineapples, coconuts, bananas, nectarines, peaches, plums, melons, guavas, grenadillas…everywhere, colour, movement, laughter, voices mingling up and down the musical scale, vocal instruments, rich in variety. I became familiar with the sing-song quality of the Mauritian: 'Ah, coco (my dear), quelle nouvelles! (What is new?). It resembled a drawl, but in fact, was more like the subtle trailing of a veil across the floor. The European women also adopted this languid manner of speaking, to begin with, then, as conversation progressed, the tempo was stepped up.

Hindu women wore the tilak on their foreheads, vivid human butterflies, as they moved about in their brilliant saris. Their men, less spectacularly dressed, gave expression to their conversations by graceful flourish of hands. The Chinese colony, not to be outdone, were delicately attired in pastel shades, or in the distinctive peacock-blue. Gaily-painted parasols provided shade from the fierce sun.

An old Indian lady near me picked up one potato after the other to examine them, then, put them back on the stall. She did this to many potatoes. I observed this behaviour with curiosity, but the trader was not amused. He lost patience. Leaning towards the offender, he bawled: 'You are breaking my head! Are you buying or not?'

The tiny woman gave him the sweetest smile, then, choosing one potato, she asked him how much he was willing to barter for it. I moved out of earshot quickly.

Vincent bought us some chilli-bites, but they proved a great disappointment, as they had no 'bite' to them at all. We went back to the vendor: "These 'gateaux piments' are not hot," Vincent told him, "'you sold them to me a short while ago."

'Not hot?' exclaimed the man, eyes widening with incredulity, 'they come out of this boiling oil.'

I intervened: 'You know very well what my husband is saying – these chilli-bites are not strong at all. We are not tourists, you know. We live here.'

The man had the grace to look abashed. He spread his hands in apologetic gesture. 'Madame, chillis are too expensive today.'

I eyed him sternly: 'And so, you trade under false pretences. That is not being honest.'

'Wait here, Madame, my brother over there, has chillies in his 'gateaux piments', I will get some for you.' The eyes implored me not to say any more on the subject, as it would give his business a bad name.

I made no further comment.

When he handed me a brown packet, fragrant with the real 'chilli-bite' mixture, I tasted one, then, nodded my approval. 'There will, of course, be no charge for these,' I told him, once again fixing him with my severe look.

'Non, non, Madame, nothing.' Adding, sotto voce: 'Sorry!'

I relented: 'Next week, when we come to Quatre Bornes, we will come to you for our 'gateaux piments'. Be sure they taste like this batch.'

He flashed me a brilliant smile.

We stopped faithfully by his stall every week. A promise is a promise.

Tiban accompanied us to Chamarel, the coloured Sands, to which tourists flock. They are truly a unique sight. Mounds of sand form small hills, reflecting different shades, mysterious veils of Nature, glinting in the sun with purple, violets, oranges, pinks, tans, reds --incredibly beautiful, spread out like an Arabian Night's texture, rich, sensuous, impacting immediately on the wonder-struck beholder.

We bought small vials, containing the glorious shades of the Chamarel sands, from the shop for Tourists there.

We could not but wonder at the incredible beauty of Nature, coming together in this one spot, to display yet another of her marvels.

Port Louis is the capital of Mauritius. There is a beautiful Park there, which contains superb specimens of water-lilies, the largest I have ever seen. They sit on their watery beds with magnificent grace, their lotus-blossoms a delight to behold, opening their pure petals in glorious shades, some so delicate, one hesitates to put a colour-name to them. Like flower-butterflies, they display their loveliness, resplendent testimony to the Harmony which sings its perfect song throughout all creation.

Looking at these giant water-lilies at 'Le Jardin des Pamplemousses' in Port Louis, I was struck with wonder. There are delightful strolls awaiting the visitor to these Gardens, where huge trees tower in majestic might, palm fronds sway in the breeze, and fragrant plants perfume the air. There is an old-world grace and symmetry in the design of these 'Jardins', an atmosphere of leisure pervades; it seems that time treads softly here. Everything appears to slow down as a mood of reverie descends from one knows not where........ voices are muted, there is a soporific influence on the senses, yet, at the same time there is a sense of heightened awareness as though anything could happen, something wholly unexpected, delightful, surprising one.

It seemed to me that the air was charged with grace, charm, peace, contentment. Tranquillity and repose settled over my soul, like a gentle hand laid in caressing gesture. Did I feel the gossamer kiss of my ancestors? Like angel-wings perhaps, had they touched me inwardly in this heavenly place where the coarse veil of mundane existence momentarily had loosened its hold on me? It was a magical spot, and I was loath to leave it.

Since my maman's death, I had not been able to identify anything as being real to me. One of my relatives took us out to sea, in an attempt to make my heart smile, but the tears were frozen icicles inside me. They could not thaw. Everything appeared to be like a postcard- picture, like a movie. I was detached from it all.

We had made friends with three workers at the Post Office. Their quaint quarters at Riviére Noire, crouched beside a giant Baobab towering over a narrow road, in close proximity to an old Churchyard, where headstones bore faint inscriptions midst the weeds and rough grasses growing everywhere. Its dishevelled look was somehow appealing, with scarlet and gold blossoms peeping boldly from their hiding places, mingling with strands of vivid bougainvillaea trailing along like bridal veils, lending colour and a fragile loveliness to the tranquil place. It was a favourite spot of mine, for dreamy strolling.

The Supervisor of this Post Office, who was a Hindu, having read my book on World Religions, arrived at our bungalow one afternoon, with an invitation from the Brahmin priest of a Hindu Temple, to be guest speaker at an important Feast in honour of the Divine Mother in Her aspect of Durga. Conscious of the honour being bestowed on me, I accepted.

Seated on the elevated platform on this religious occasion, I beheld the human flowers spread out below me like a gorgeous Fan, as women wearing saris of all colours, graced the gathering. Eager-faced children sat attentively, shining eyes alert with anticipation. The men were impeccably groomed, taking their places with dignified mien.

I thought the Hindu greeting was very beautiful, as heads bowed before the joined hands in 'Namaskar', at heart-level. It reminded me of the words used by the author L. Adams Beck: 'In the unity of the Divine, we meet again...' For, is not every meeting a divinely-planned occasion?

Sandalwood incense filled the air, the Brahmin priests who were to my right on the podium, began a sonorous chanting. Then, there was attentive silence as the congregations centred their attention on the passages from the Ramayana, which followed. One priest read a part of the great, Sacred Epic, then, he waited, as the second priest explained the inner meaning of the passage to his rapt listeners.

Time passed. As clouds of incense billowed about me, I felt as though I was floating away from the world. There arose before me the face of my maman, who had so recently left me behind on her journey to the Stars...deep within me, I knew she had not gone anywhere, that the NOW is ever present, and that it is the ego which gives rise to foolish imaginings. I felt peace enfold me, as maman's presence embraced me. Mother reveals Herself to me as ISNESS – beyond the grasp of mind...the heart alone, can receive the mystery of LOVE.

A hand touched my arm. I looked up to see the Brahmin priest smiling gravely at me. It was time to talk about Mother.

I had prepared no notes. I spoke from my heart. Power, peace, a serene flow of words poured forth.......Mother, in all Her aspects, was my adoration. It was so simple to speak about so familiar, so well-beloved a treasure!

The Brahmin priest came to my side when I fell silent, his face was wreathed in smiles. Having bowed to me, and accompanied me to my former place on the podium, he said to his congregation: 'This wise lady has said in a few minutes what I have taken years to teach. The essence was all there in the words she handed to you.'

My heart was happy, to hear him say this.

After the service, I and my husband, were invited to the Head Priest's house, where we were given prasad (blessed food), and warm milk laced with honey, to drink. It was a fitting end to a memorable evening. I felt very humble at having been so privileged.

Regarding the religious history of Mauritius, one could go back to the seventeenth and eighteen centuries, where the Lazaristes first came as Missionaries to l'Ile de France (Mauritius), and l' Ile de Bourbon (Reunion). It was hard going for the Lazaristes, with a population made up of Europeans who were lax in religious affairs, and black slaves imported from Mozambique, Madagascar and other places, who were more inclined to follow the bad example of the Whites, rather than follow the counsel and teachings of the priests.

The India Company, who held sway over the islands, did not bother itself too much with fulfilling its obligations of building churches, schools, presbyteries.

Whereas five hundred houses had been built for the Whites of French origin, religious edifices were neglected altogether.

In 1756, one church was finally built, to which only the Europeans were admitted, and those few who attended, came only on Sunday.

During the French Revolution, the Lazaristes returned to France. They were replaced by priests who were, for the most part, poor examples of how Missionaries should conduct themselves, neglecting even to baptize infants.

In 1810, the Island was taken over by the British, and its name was changed back to Mauritius, originally given to it, by the Dutch, in honour of Maurice of Nassau.

Pope Pius V11 in 1820, sent as envoy to the Island, Monsignor Slatter, who was succeeded eleven years later, by Monsignor Morriss. Finally, Monsignor Collier arrived, accompanied by four priests, to evangelize 80,000 souls! It was, to say the least, a difficult task.

And now, there appeared on the scene, the best-loved saint of Mauritius, Père Laval. His story merits to be told. In a former written work, Père Laval appears like a shining star, but I shall repeat a sketch of his life here, for the reader's edification.

Jacques Desiré Laval, was born in Normandy, on the 18th September 1803. His father was Mayor of Croth, in the diocese of Evreux. The name of his mother, was Suzanne.

The Laval couple were deeply religious, sheltering ten to fifteen paupers at a time, in their family home. Suzanne Laval died when Jacques was but eight years old. She left ten orphans, the eldest of whom had barely seen thirteen summers.

From having been a sunny-natured child, Jacques became reflective and quiet after his mother's death. He carried this profound sadness with him for another thirty years; then, just as the sunshine pierces the clouds, his happy nature reasserted itself. When Jacques was eleven years old, he was entrusted to the care of his uncle. Abbé Laval, parish priest of Tourville – La Campagne.

Jacques's father wanted him to choose a studious career. The Abbé counselled against this course, fearing that the child's timid and retiring nature would suffer from the harshness of College life. An alternative decision was taken, and Jacques was sent to the Seminary at Evreux. It proved to be a disaster. The thin youth of fifteen, became even more introspective, withdrawing into himself and conceiving a dislike for study. Never robust, his health became even more fragile. Within him, the silent grieving for his mother intensified.

Irritated, his father brought him home, where he put him to work in the fields. It was hard going, and Jacques's eldest sister was often at this side to lend a helping hand, ever ready to encourage him. A second attempt at the Seminary proved negative, so Jacques was packed off to the Stanislaus College in Paris. There, the youth suddenly blossomed, evincing a keen interest in his studies, and enjoying his first successful results, to the relief of his father and uncle.

In 1826, he was awarded the Diploma of Bachelor of Science. He decided on a medical career. After four years of study, he presented his thesis entitled: 'An Essay on Articulary Rheumatism.'

Intending to practise as an Intern at a Hospital, Jacques was prevented from doing so, by the arrival of the 'carabins' who sought him out, to see that he discharged his military duties. Eluding them, he walked all the way to Normandy, arriving there totally exhausted.

In September 1830, Doctor Laval took up a post at Saint André, near Evreux, where he was already known to both rich and poor. The latter lost no time in flocking to him; for, not only did the doctor not charge them a fee, but he also saw to it that they received hot food, bread, and wine.

It was not long, before the Pharmacist in the town, and the doctor already established there, declared war on the new arrival, who was far too popular for their liking. They made life so difficult for the young Doctor, that he moved to Ivry-la-Bataille. As the doctor there, was on the point of going into retirement, things augured well for young Doctor Laval, who was known to the townspeople, having relatives living there.

The young doctor dressed in the height of fashion, well-cut trousers, jacket with silk lapels, a cravat round the neck, and a top hat of the latest Chateaubriand- style, on his head. He danced well, was a good horseman, owned a smart coach and horses. To all appearances, he was a very successful young man.

Some things however, did not change. The poor were not charged a fee, with the result that the doctor worked until his eyes closed with fatigue. He paid no heed to acquiring wealth, had no desire to marry. Within him, inner voices made themselves heard: 'You are mad! You work too hard. You must change your ways…find a more solid foundation, so that you can truly help your fellow-creatures.'

He began to pay more and more attention to these inner counsels, with the result that his life-style changed. The dandy disappeared. Former Cordon Bleu meals, were replaced by simple fare. The carafes of wine were seen no more at his table. Water became his drink.

People began to talk: 'A pious doctor? This is not possible, surely?'

One day, the doctor was returning home, when his horse fell into a ditch, and was killed instantly. Its rider was pinned beneath him. The shock of the accident turned the young man's thoughts inward, forcing him to focus on his inner state. It resulted in his entering the Seminary of Saint Sulpice at the age of thirty-two. Here, he subjected himself to severe austerities. Once, in the heart of winter, he saw a shivering mendicant by the roadside. With gentle hands, he placed his coat about the man's shoulders, and went his way. When at home for the holidays, Jacques slept on a straw pallet, enfolding himself in his doctor's cape. He spent long hours on his knees in prayer, leaving bloody tracks on the cold floor tiles. He was received into the Priesthood on the 2nd December, 1838.

Two months later, he was sent as Curé, to the village of Pinterville, where the villagers were lax in the practice of their religion. Undaunted, Pére Laval armed himself with the indomitable weapon of prayer, and rose every morning at four, to pray for his flock. At first, the priest's parishioners paid no heed to the silvery song of the Church bells, as they heralded the celebration of Holy Mass, but it was not long before they began referring their Curé, as 'that saintly man.'

Pére Laval busied himself in his small Church, sweeping, dusting, scrubbing the floors, painting inside and outside walls. He gathered wild flowers from the fields, arranged them in vases, and spread them in artful fashion upon the pure, white linen he had placed upon the altar. Silver candlesticks gleamed, polished like mirrors, the tall candles cast a soft, radiant light on the place of worship. Clad in his priestly vestments, Pére Laval stood at the Church door, awaiting his flock, a smile of welcome on his lips.

The village school had no teacher, so Pére Laval took upon himself this work, gathering around him about twelve pupils. Many youngsters worked at the factory of Louviers, from 6 a.m. to 9 p.m. It was not long before the poor from outlying districts, converged on Pinterville, where Pére Laval held night classes, giving religious instruction. The Curé fed the poor who came to him, in his kitchen, delighted to see them. 'I am with the best friends of Our Lord,' he would say, watching his visitors eat.

Pére Laval visited the sick, remaining on his knees in their presence all the while. Once, when the river Eure, was in flood, he knelt on his horse's back, to save those in the water. Again and again, he went back, to pull someone to safety. He gave shelter to numerous families rendered homeless by the disaster.

A few months later, Père Laval was told that he was being sent to the Island of Mauritius. He accepted.

On the 25th September 1841, Pére Laval stepped on to Mauritian soil. The heat hit him like a fist. The gentle breeze floating in from the Indian Ocean's azure waters, did little to cool the air. Ex-slaves lolled about, listless in the heat, avid eyes fixed on the new arrivals, hopeful hands held out in timeless begging-gesture.

The priest did not need long to realize that his colleagues who had been sent out to help, had indeed sadly neglected their duties. In a letter Father

Liberman, he wrote: 'The priests up till now have not troubled themselves with the poor people, in fact, they have treated them as though they were animals – and yet, there is much good that can be done for them. If we had done for them what we had done for the Whites, our work would have been efficient...the priests have given unimaginable scandal...and here is the wound. The deep wound of this poor island of Mauritius. Few marry – they go from one relationship to another with ease...they abandon themselves to drunkenness...the young women are debauched by their masters and white youth – those born here, called Creoles are corrupt. I am working with some poor Malgaches, (Blacks from Madagascar), and several Mozambicans.'

Although about half of the Black on the Island had been baptised, in Pére Laval's eyes, they lived like pagans. Slavery had been abolished in 1839, but for most of the ex-slaves, freedom meant having nothing to do, that is, starving to death. They found field work repellent, associating it with the Overseer's whip. Many of the Blacks brought to the island on slave-ships, could not even speak one word of Créole. To survive, there remained only begging or brigandry. But now, for the very first time, the Blacks of Mauritius could claim a priest for their very own; one who actually cared about their welfare, who spoke of loving them. Could this be truly possible? Pére Laval began his mission in Mauritius as he had done in Pinterville. He went down on his knees and prayed. He lived close to the Presbytery in a two-roomed hut. There, he slept in his trunk, which led to the belief that he took his rest in a coffin. At 3.30 a.m. he was up, celebrating Holy Mass an hour later. His first meal was at noon, which consisted only of rice. At noon, he ate only rice. The evening meal was bread and eggs.

Pére Laval continued to undergo severe austerities. He became very thin, causing his superiors much concern. The priest learnt to speak Créole, in order to be more acceptable to the Blacks. Within six months, he was proficient in this 'pretty language' as he called it. Wherever he went, Pére Laval rubbed shoulders with the extremely poor, especially among the Blacks. In contrast to the 'golden lives' of the Whites, seated under their large parasols on the beaches, sipping iced drinks brought to them by their servants, the squalor, filth, and suffering of the poor, touched the priest's heart, wounding him deeply. He spent long hours watching malaria ravage young and old, alike, as it caused sweating, shivering, and high fevers. Black-water fever struck fiercely at unexpected moments. Pot-bellied children stood in doorway, their huge eyes filled with suffering, whilst their sorrowful mothers clutched at them. Men lolled about in the shade, many in drunken stupor, others with lack-lustre eyes, stared at the priest in their midst in his black soutane. Pére Laval wept for these neglected children of the Church, of humanity!

One day, Pére Laval declared from the pulpit, that he would celebrate a special Mass only for his Black parishioners, at noon every Sunday. This announcement caused a sensation in Port Louis. The Europeans were amused. The Blacks could not believe their ears. The Pére won their hearts. For the first time in their lives, they were being treated with kindness, with consideration – as though they were people! There was no arrogance, only a sincere cordiality from the priest. His feelings for them sprang from a humble, pure heart. They stared unbelievingly as their priest. For the first time in their lives, they were being treated with kindness, with consideration – as though they were people! There was no arrogance, only a sincere cordiality from the priest. His feelings for them sprang from a humble, pure heart. They were deeply moved when Pére Laval touched them on the arm, tapped a shoulder, made the Sign of the Cross, on a forehead, handed out clothes, food, sweets. Their whole lives became lit up like a beacon. The Blacks would have done anything for this extraordinary man.

At noon, the heat in Mauritius is truly terrific. It is that hour in the Tropics, when the Hibiscus closes her petals, the smallest breeze does not stir leaf or blossom. The air is suffocating, the sun blinding. When the Whites went to Church in Port Louis, the Blacks were relegated to the back, separated by a balustrade, which they were forbidden to touch. It was this noon hour, which Pére Laval chose to celebrate his special Mass. So intense is the heat, that he knew the Whites would not attend. So, sensibilities remained intact, and the Blacks could occupy all the rows in the Church. One day, the balustrade disappeared, and was never seen again.

After some time had elapsed, converts increased. One day, Pére Laval was sent to L'ile de Bourbon (Reunion), by his Superiors, for a well-earned rest, as his health was causing concern.

Soon, the priest returned to Mauritius. He resumed his gruelling routine. One night, the priest saw a man standing at the back of the Church, with a stout rope about his waist. The Pére took him in hand. 'Emilien,' he told the man, 'follow God and follow me.' From that hour, Emilien was the priest's shadow, proving especially useful in his ministry with the poor in the Valley of the Priests, were since the days of slavery, these unfortunates were classified as semi -primitives. Pére Laval addressed them thus: 'if you fear me, here is Emilien who will speak in my place.'

Obediently, Emilien gave them spiritual instruction. Soon, this unique evangelization of Blacks by Blacks, spread, and a grand conversion took place all over the island. Chapels began to appear, rising in spontaneous response to the need of the people. By October 1847, Pére Laval wrote that a dozen chapels had been built around Port Louis, made of wood, and rather 'lovely'. Birds settled on the rafters, sending out their musical accompaniments from their high perches. A few months later, twenty chapels greeted the swelling ranks of Church-goers.

But now, calamity struck the Island. In March 1854, cholera killed some prisoners. By the end of May, more than six hundred had died, to be followed by a further four hundred in the space of a week. Panic gripped the populace. There was a frantic exodus from the capital, as residents fled to outlying districts. Long columns of pall-bearers were seen in cemeteries, as the death toll mounted.

Pére Laval organized Nursing Groups in sections of the town. The epidemic lasted three months, during which time Pére Laval worked incessantly, supervising his Groups, hearing confessions, tending the sick, administering the last rites to the dying, comforting the bereaved, organizing meals for the indigent, celebrating Holy Mass, giving spiritual instruction, beside carrying out his other pastoral duties such as baptising and performing marriages.

The grim statistics unfolded. In Port Louis alone, there were more than thirty deaths daily. The old people and orphans were taken to Montagne Longue, where families adopted them. Then, suddenly, it was over. The cholera left as swiftly as it had arrived.

Pére Laval did not forget the prisoners. In his worn soutane, wearing an old hat, and carrying his parasol, he was a familiar sight as he entered the prison to care for his 'poor children behind bars'.

People stared at the frail priest seated in the cart of infamy, beside the condemned prisoners on their way to their execution. He encouraged and sustained them to the last, remaining close to the scaffold where he could be present until the final moments.

Pére Laval fell ill in 1864. He said: 'What happiness to have been in the midst of the poor of Our Lord. What a good idea I had, to work with the Poor. I bless the good Lord. I thank Him.'

Pére Laval died on 9th September, 1864.

■■

I had heard my father speak reverently of this gentle Saint of Mauritius, and I asked Pére Laval to protect Mimou, Mamushka, and her three grown children, as we bade them adieu.

Mamushka had taken Mimou on training sorties, so that I knew he would be able to survive when we had left the island, nevertheless, tears poured down my face as I was driven away to the airport. I had prepared lots of food for my cat-children, and my cousin Janine, had promised to keep an eye out for them, but I was under no illusions, life would be grim for them without us.

With my maman's death, our plans for life on Mauritius had been drastically altered.

We returned to London. There, I befriended a gaunt, black cat, whose amber eyes were haunted by a sadness which tore at me whenever I saw her treading with delicate, hesitant step across the wooden fence. She appeared one morning, soon after our arrival, like a mist of fur, as if from nowhere, to stare at me with wary look. She was so thin, she floated like a cloud, one which would disintegrate at any moment, I thought.

I placed food and drink for this starving apparition, who had been put on my 'Way' to be cared for to the best of my ability........very slowly, as though every step hurt, the bundle of cat-hood moved towards the food. When she jumped to the ground I realized she was indeed very ill, as she swayed, righted herself, then proceeded to narrow the distance between herself and food.

I entered the kitchen so as to let her eat in peace. Although she was desperately hungry, my visitor ate with delicate grace, stopping to drink in between nibbles, her tiny head ever on the look-out even as she ate. When she had finished, I stood in the doorway, talking to her, sending love-waves through the air, hoping that healing vibrations from my heart would help the starved and hurt animal before me. She looked at me with wonder, as though kindness and gentleness was totally foreign to her: 'Poor little one,' I said to her, 'have you never heard soft words before? Never mind, you can come here whenever you like, there will be food and drink waiting for you. I shall not harm you or chase you away. God bless you, my little one.'

Tears misted my sight. The cat looked so forlorn, so alone! Today was the first meeting. Hopefully, she would put on weight, lose that haunted look. She limped away, managed an awkward leap on to the fence, then, she was gone.

Next day her tiny face peered from the far end of the garden. I called to her, showed her food and drink.

She came.

I was delighted.

Presently, I was able to coax her to eat twice a day. Gradually, she put on weight, but the limp remained with her, as did the haunted look in her eyes, which told of past suffering not forgotten. She became more confident with time, having considered that I posed no threat to her, but that did not mean she could relax in human company. Humans are not always humane!

My heart ached to see this tiny morsel of cat-hood so severely wounded, both inside and out, but I could do no more than give her regular meals, and send out love-bouquets to her. One day, she would leave this world to race across a heavenly expanse with Joy as companion. There has never been the slightest doubt in my mind that animals do not grace Heaven, with their beauty and innocence. The heart is wise, it KNOWS. This is why the Mysteries emphasis the need for Heart-Understanding as opposed to Cerebral Intelligence only. Did not King Solomon the Wise, ask God for an Understanding Heart?

There will always be those who denigrate animal-lovers, dismissing them as 'sentimental fools', scoffing at our tender concern for our 'dumb friends', yet this is not to be wondered at, for, as we know full well, fruits mature in their own time – so too, will Human-fruit!

The next pilgrim to my door was of a dark-grey shade, whose one eye had been hurt at one time. She sat on my kitchen-step, waiting for me to appear. No doubt, she had observed Black Mist limping to her dish every day, and had now decided to come to this special place herself. Who can guess what amount of courage, of sheer guts, this coming out into the open, call for, in an animal? Yet, here she was, hoping........soon, he dish was set before her, as were her milk and water.

For the period we stayed in London, Black Mist and Brave Girl were our guest, then, once more, destiny took me away. Tears, prayers, blessings.

Life is a perpetual 'hello' and 'good-bye'.

Islam means total submission to the Will of God. The Christian learns to say: 'Thy Will be done.'

To love means to expose the heart to the wounding of parting, but it is a wounding which mysteriously confers with every tear, ever greater nobility and richness of spirit.

Love is to be approached on bended knee, with awe, with reverence, for in that Sacred Presence, the soul trembles before so great a secret! A secret, the mind can never hope to penetrate. I once wrote:

'The Weaving of Destiny, it must be told,
Fashions a Cloth of shimmering gold.
Cleverly hidden from mortal sight
By the bewitching power of Maya's might.
Magically, things are not what they seem,
Caught in the 'I' of a Cosmic Dream.
The whys and wherefores are Mystery,
For God is the Weaver of Destiny.'

I know that tears are part of the human fabric – there is no escape from them. Somewhere, within my inner landscapes, there is a Sacred Rainbow which never fades, and all those animals I have loved, and love still, dance on this Rainbow, for they too, can never vanish.......and so, I surrender to the All-Wise.

* * * * * * * * * * * * * *

Why do birds sing?
The are love-notes
From the Heart of God.

- The Author

Our stay in Morocco was a short one, then, we were off again.

When we finally settled, we were nearing Retirement Age, my husband and I, so we chose a quiet cottage in the countryside.

Refurbishing occupied many months, but I had time to sit on my Inner Rainbow with my loved ones, enjoying the ecstatic joy of inner togetherness! In such moments, I would recall many things.

The day for instance, when I had knelt by the side of a swimming pool in France, on a visit to my brother Francis and his wife, Winifred. I had been absorbed in saving struggling insects from the water, when, unbeknown to me, someone had made fun of my behaviour, whereupon my brother had rushed to my defence, then, had jumped fully-clad into the pool, shouting: 'I am coming to help you, sis,' holding a net in one hand. Ignoring the amazed stares of other Restaurant diners, he had proceeded to do just that. Wonderful brother of mine!

On another occasion, I got out of my car in Johannesburg to jump on to a cart where an African was whipping a horse with such cruel power that the animal, who was obviously very sick, covered as he was, in sores on his gaunt body, staggered. Furious with the man, I snatched the whip out of his hand: 'Stop that, you tsotsi!' (bandit).

I was so angry I could have caught fire. By this time, other motorists came to my side, curious to see why this woman blazed with such fury. I asked one of them to contact the S.P.C.A., whilst another man called the police. In those days, there was a unit called the 'Flying Squad', and true to their name, these members of the Law were on the scene in no time. I still held the whip, which I relinquished to a tall policeman with eyes of iron-grey.

'You can step down, lady,' he said to me.

'Don't give that man this whip,' I told him, as I jumped down to the road.

'No fear of that. This skelm (ruffian) is staying right here.'

'Thank you,' was my reply, adding 'I am also staying right here, until the S.P.C.A. people get here.'

The policeman's mouth twitched, as he fought off a smile: 'Then, just move your car, please.'

'Will do.'

Having parked my Taunus, I waited near the cart, watching the three members of the Flying Squad Team questioning the sullen-faced African.

Presently, a van came alongside, a figure stepped out. The man from the S.P.C.A. made straight for the horse, as I did.

That day was a good day! The horse was immediately taken under the wing of kindly souls, and whisked away to the Animal Refuge. I was content.

In recent years, there had been a close shave with a snake when my sister Jacqueline and her husband Jan, had taken me to the Kruger Park with Jean-Pierre, their son.

We had spent an exciting day viewing wild animals in their natural habitat, now, we were putting the finishing touches to our evening meal which was to be eaten under the stars.

Jacqueline, Jean-Pierre and myself, were beside the dining table, when Jan walked over from the Grill-area. He said in a surprised voice: 'There is a snake here!'

'Where?'

Three people lost no time in jumping on to chairs. Jan went to get a long poker. With this, he tried to coax the snake to come out of its hiding place, but he met with no success. The snake burrowed under the door-mat which was made of rattan.

'Go and get help, Jan,' his wife told him.

Obediently, Jan went towards the Main Dining Room, returning a short while later, accompanied by a young woman armed with a long rod, at the end of which, dangled a noose.

When she saw us standing on chairs, she smiled in amusement. And she was right. Did we think we were safe from our unwelcome visitor there! Panic does not reason – and we were most definitely panic-stricken.

Very calmly and politely, she asked us to move to some distance. We obeyed with alacrity.

The young woman then proceeded, very cautiously, to move away the matting. We all cried out as she sprang back. She sounded an epithet I will not repeat here, but which, under the circumstances, was perfectly normal, because the snake had made a lightning move in her direction, as though sensing her preoccupation in shifting him. Again, she dangled the noose close to the moving head. Success! This time she had him.

'You are not going to kill him?' I called out.

The woman flashed me a smile: 'Never! I will set him free when I reach the fence.'

Off she went, with the snake firmly held.

We breathed a sigh of relief.

I once watched a snake being killed, some years back, and it had pained me grievously, because there had been absolutely no need for it to suffer such a fate at all.

Near the Magaliesberg Mountains, there are delightful retreats, where one can spend a few days' relaxation, far from the madding crowd. The area is very beautiful, retaining a wild, rugged look which has its special charm.

This particular week-end, I had walked over to the Restaurant to have my evening meal. I was seated on the terrace overlooking gentle hills from whence came the barking coughs of male baboons placed as sentinels on their look-out posts. The troop was returning homewards after a day in the nearby forest. In leisurely fashion, they were making their way to higher ground for the night, babies like jockeys, seated on their mothers' backs.

Suddenly, there was a commotion below the dining area. I joined the other guests to see what was causing these loud shouts. Three African staff had discovered a snake making its way across the stone paving. Having armed themselves with stout sticks, they were clubbing it to death, screaming whilst thus occupied.

Shocked and saddened by the sight, I walked away, my enjoyment of the night shattered by this brutal act, for, it is well known that snakes love to lie in hot places, as this unfortunate reptile had done. It was obvious that he had been returning to the undergrowth, when his presence had been detected. A few seconds more, and he would have reached safety, - humans had decided otherwise.

Early next morning, I arose at dawn, walked over to where I had seen the dead snake disposed of, and, under the curious gaze of the African staff busy cleaning the premises, I opened the dustbin to retrieve the snake from its unacceptable grave.

I carried the bloody corpse to my Rondavel, where I placed it in the bath tub. I washed the entire body, still so cruelly marked by its violent end.

Then, I placed it into some cloth I had ready for that purpose, and, holding the snake in my arms, I walked some distance from human habitation, till I reached a spot I thought would be free of 'vandals'.

I gently unwound the cloth, removed the battered body, once so supple and beautiful, and laid it down beside wild flowers and fragrant grasses.

Here was its place, I thought, back in Mother Nature's arms, close to her Earthy Heart, so full of starlight...

As I stood looking at my snake, I meditated on the Egyptian Uraeus, mighty secret symbol of Wisdom. To the Ancients, the snake was representative of the vital centre of respiration; its trajectory of which vital Fire is evoked by the shape of the spinal column. It is this rising of this victorious Sacred Fire-Energy towards the crown of the head which is symbolised by the Pharoanic Uraeus.

The Egyptian iart – oart – is derived from the root, iar or oar, signifying 'to rise'. The cobra does this with his 'raised' hood – just as the Serpent-Fire mounts along the spinal column to become triumphant Wisdom-Pharoah!

This universal archetypal symbol, was widely dispersed throughout the ancient world, where the snake was a dynamic symbol of life energy and regeneration, and seen as a benevolent, not, an evil force.

The author, Arthur Osborne, devoted follower of the Sage of Arunachala, recounts: 'Bhagavan (The Sage), would not have snakes killed where he resided. "We have come to their home and have no right to trouble or disturb them. They do not molest us." And they did not. Once, his mother was frightened when a cobra approached her. Sri Bhagavan walked towards it, and it turned and went away. It passed between two rocks and he followed it. However, the passage ended against a rock-wall and, unable to escape, the snake turned and coiled its body and looked at him. The Sage also looked. This continued for some minutes and then the cobra uncoiled and feeling no more need for fear, crawled quietly away, passing close to his feet.' 4

The difference between Wisdom and ignorance!

I was made aware of the beauty about me. The sky wore robes of glory, lighting up the Magaliesberg Range nearby, sending shafts of sunlight through the woodlands like golden arrows falling to earth.

My snake blazed with amber splendour... Peace kissed my soul. All was well.

*　　　*　　　*

The Mystic And The Beggar

================================

God give you a good day, my friend, said the Mystic.
I thank God I never had a bad day, said the Beggar.
God give you a happy life, said the Mystic.
I thank God I am never unhappy, said the Beggar.
But who are you? Asked the Mystic,
surprised by his reply.
I am a king, said the Beggar.
But where is your kingdom? said the Mystic.
To whom the Beggar once again answered,
In my own heart.

....

When my maternal grandmother was very ill, we kept watch at her bedside in turns.

Grandmère Maya's large, green eyes would regard me steadily: 'How much do you love me?' she would ask.

I knew the reply she wanted to hear: 'like the sky – like the sea,' I answered.

She smiled, content.

The day before her death, her hand plucked nervously at the coverlet. I took them in my own.

It is all right, Grandmère, I am here.'

She sank back deeper into the pillows, closed her eyes, only for a moment, then, they were open again, but this time happiness, wonderment, joy, shone from them. Suddenly, she leaned forward, took her hands from my clasp, and slapped them against her knees, calling out the names of her pets who had died: 'Come, come, Bijou – BouBoel, Flye…come, come.' Then, a laugh of sheer delight as her hands fondled pets which were not visible to me, but whom grandmother knew were there.

Next, she peered at a spot over my right shoulder. A sigh escaped her lips, a whisper: 'It is you...' Then, she uttered a name I had never heard before, but which my maman told me later, was the pet name grandmère Maya had given her husband. She had been a widow for fifty-eight years!

I was present when these extraordinary events took place.

Those beloved pets Grandmère had so loved, had come to accompany her to Heaven. Her romantic Prince whom she had never forgotten or stopped loving, had come to take her to the Love-Realm.

Back in our quiet retreat, my husband and I were learning to adapt to being Senior Citizens, those strange people, who suddenly, for some reason or other, are seen by many as having descended from one day to the next, to a 'different' level. From being a working professional one is 'demoted' being a 'Pensioner', where the brain-power, working at steady pace for so many years, is thought to falter. Words like 'old age' or 'ageing process' is glibly applied when one faces medical persons. Then, the standard phrase: 'One must expect this at your age, you know...'

'No, doctor, I do not know. Yesterday, I was part of the vigorous working force, faithfully paying up all the taxes demanded of me – today, suddenly, I have become a' 'drain on the economy', and for some of you among the medical profession, I am no doubt, an "expendable commodity' from whom expensive drugs must be withheld. Well, I have news for you. I have no intention of rolling over, of playing 'dead' – on the contrary, I am going to study all those things I have not had enough time to devote myself to whilst being one of society's Beavers. I am going to keep this mind of mine honed to such a pitch, that you will have trouble keeping up with me.'

It never ceases to amaze me how our society (in general), views older people.

We were brought up to show respect and have regard for, the older generation. When our grandmothers walked into the room, we stood up as a mark of our esteem. In fact, we were delighted to have our Senior Citizens present at parties or receptions. Grandmère Maya played the piano, as did her sister, Aunt Ines. Our uncle Robert told funny stories. Aunt Miriam sang in her superb contralto, and papa regaled us with his rich, tenor voice. The entire family joined in games after dinner, Charade, being one of the favourites. There was none of this shunting aside of the elderly one sees so often today.

The ancients held the older generation in high esteem, coming to them for counsel, eager to learn from their life-experience.

Whatever labels an ignorant society may place upon mature people, will not alter the fact that the most delicious wines are those past the youthful stage, that the most beautiful leaf is the one flaming with the brilliant shades of glorious Autumn...

To those men and women who are Senior Citizens, I say: 'Youth – that Immortal Elixir, is the Heart. The ageing of the physical cannot touch this Sacred Realm. It lies beyond the reach of ignorant humans who worship outer youth, outer beauty, outer success. Happily, this Secret Kingdom which is ageless because timeless, is free – accessible to us all. Hold your heads high! Walk with regal step. We have come a long way to get where we are. Be patient with those who discard us so casually – they will learn.

And now, it was time to play parents again to the animal-people.

One morning, a neighbour came to our gate on a bicycle. Tucked under each arm was a tiny bundle of fur.

'My daughter brought me this brother and sister a few days ago. Do you want them?'

We held out our hands.

Zig and Zag entered our lives.

They had long hair, shaded buff, grey and black. Their eyes varied from light green to a lovely amber. There was the usual flurry to buy the necessary baskets, cat litter, food - dishes and so on.

The kittens gazed about them in wonder, two puffs of cotton wool which moved.

Zig, the female, was brave, adventurous, wise. Her brother, Zag, was cautious, prone to sounding off high, plaintive calls whenever apprehensive, definitely not so daring as his sister.

At night, they curled up on our beds, never stirring till morning. Because they had just been weaned, I sewed two special coats for them with their names embroidered on the cloth, to which I affixed long tapes. With these coats on, Zig and Zag were brought outside, where the long tapes were tied firmly to a large rock in the garden.

Zag got himself entangled about a rose-bush. Next, he went round and round like a whirling Dervish, causing a sapling to break in two. We put them somewhere else, after a comforting saucer of milk to settle their nerves.

This time, Zig decided to explore the undercarriage of our car. She was disentangled, brought inside for a shampoo, screaming for her mother who, happened to be a terrible foster-parent on two legs.

Weeks passed.

One morning I walked over to get something from the shed. Lo and behold, Zag dangled from the window ledge. I rushed to his rescue. He used to lie down whenever we wanted to take him across the lawn, uttering strange gurgles of protests, not at all sounds dignified cats usually make.

Then, the coats came off. It was time. I put butter on the small paws, asked Padre Pio to protect them, then, sent them off into the garden, with trepidation.

My husband and I watched with bated breath, as they tore about in uncontrolled glee, sprinting this way, then that, as though demented, intoxicated by their new-found freedom. My heart was in my mouth as they dashed across the road, back home again, then, off into the road once more. I could not watch. I went inside.

I need not have worried with Padre Pio casting his special protective eye on them. When they grew weary, the explorers returned, tails high in the air, like the banners of conquering heroes. We made the appropriate sounds which meant welcome, congratulations, we are so proud of you. Two small heads bent over their food dish, pink tongues drank thirstily. What an adventure! Soon, they collapsed on the sofa, utterly spent.

Our cat-children developed wonderfully well, with Zag acquiring his special saunter which I called the 'John Wayne' stride. Zig was regal always, head held erect, strong paws pacing evenly in slow, determined fashion. She could, however, astound, when she became suddenly transformed into an Impala, racing along, then, leaping and bounding with remarkable speed and agility.

One of her favourite hiding places was an old roof-shed across the road from our cottage. There, she would sit, looking down at us with her star-eyes, whilst we called her to come in at bedtime. We were all the more concerned for her safety every since the ear infection she had developed, before she came to us, had caused her to become deaf. With the imperturbable air which cats assume, known so well to all feline lovers, Zig remained impervious to our pleading gestures from below, regarding us calmly, without moving from her chosen vantage point. After a few such sorties, we resigned ourselves to allowing her Majesty to make her way home when she wished.

Then, as though in sympathy for my husband, who had broken his hip, Zig came home one day, trailing one leg behind her. She disappeared into a kitchen cupboard which was on ground level, and which had been left slightly ajar. No amount of coaxing would induce her to leave the spot which she had chosen to convalesce in. She ate and drank inside the cupboard, her large, luminous eyes signalling us to let her be.

When she came out, eventually, she limped. The Vet told us that her hip had been hurt, but that it had healed as well as it ever could. Every since, she has remained with that slight limp.

Perhaps a year later, she developed a swelling in her right side which proved to be an abscess. She was operated upon, and healed well.

Zag sauntered happily about, not accident - prone, it would appear, like his sister. He did however, develop mange. Happily, this is curable these days, and after a few weeks' treatment, he was rid of it.

Poor Zig was not out of the wars yet. Too curious, she investigated a ferret lying low somewhere, to her cost. It gave her a nasty bite on the mouth, which took some time to heal.

Finally, her fearlessness against marauders cost her a nasty wound under her right eye, which became infected. The Vet gave me antibiotics for her, and she was soon well again.

An illness in the family, brought me to Johannesburg, where I received the surprise visit of our Zulu gardener Tatti Dlomo. I was delighted to see him. He was working as a gardener for the Anglo-Vaal Corporation, where a reference I had given him on behalf of my parents, had obtained him the job.

'Miss Gladys, I am so-ooo glad to see you. So many years now, since I saw you.'

He still had a youthful face, but his eyes were those of a warrior, tested by suffering. Although he gave me a lovely smile, his eyes remained sad.

'You know, Miss Gladys (Tatti paid no heed to my marital status), I got married.'

'Tatti! That is wonderful!'

The pain in his eyes burst through like a thunderclap.

'She died.'

'Oh, Tatti. I am so sorry. What happened. Tell me.'

I took his hands in mine, as I had done in the past, whenever Tatti had known trouble.

His voice took on reverent tones, as he told me his story; 'My mother always liked this one girl who lived in the next village. When I came home on a visit, my mother, she tells me: "Tatti, she is a star. You should think about what I say. When I die, who will be here for you to cheer your heart when you come from the fields? You must not live in an empty house. You must hear laughter, happiness. This, I want for you. Listen to your mother, and go and pay court to this girl. Her eyes follow you with love. You must talk about lobola (bride - price) with her father.

"Well, I went to see this girl, and I liked her very much. So, I arranged for the lobola, and we got married.'

I released his hands, to pour the tea and place a slice of cake on a plate. These, I handed to Tatti.

'Yes, those were good times. My wife was very happy, always laughing – she was dancing also. My mother told me she was glad, because now when she died, her son had someone who loved him. Aie! But she got pregnant, my wife, and I was so worried, because out there, Miss Gladys, we are far away from the doctors. Something here (he touched his heart), was not right. Do you remember how I told you, Miss Gladys, how my people believe there is a big snake in the river that calls women, and then they die? I felt like that, Miss Gladys. Yes, something was wrong! I told my mother to be very careful, to watch over my wife specially…I came back to Johannesburg, but still this thing would not go away, so I asked my Boss to let me go home when my wife was going to have the baby. The Boss said it was all right. Now, I take the train, I come home, I am worried, but my wife is there, laughing, and my mother is saying that all young husbands are the same, not trusting the women to deliver babies safely: "Tatti", my mother says to me, "my son, don't be foolish. Do you not see how the cows go about their business so well. Where are the bulls when all these calves are being born, eh?"

And so, we all laugh together. Then, the day comes. The pains start. I call the man who is to take us to the Hospital, but it is far. We get into the car, my mother also. My wife is screaming. I am holding her.'

Tatti paused, stared hard at me, as though wanting to imprint those terrible hours on my heart also, so as to share his anguish, even in small measure.

The soft voice resumes the narrative, but now in a sing-song fashion, as though the tongue obeys like mechanical function: 'My wife asked me to take away the pain. I can see by my mother's face, that this is not right. It is too early for such screaming, she tells me. But still, my wife shouts, struggling in my arms. I want to help her, but I can do nothing.'

And now, tears slide down Tatti's cheeks. With quick gesture he flicks them away. They keep coming. He bows his head.

My heart is riven. I remain very still.

A storm of sobbing overtakes Tatti. I go across to where he sits, cradle his head gently. So much pain! Where has the laughing, carefree youth who once came to me with exercise books in hand, gone? Oh, where has this Rainbow-Tatti gone?

Here, instead, was a man scarred with suffering.

It was some time before Tatti could continue with his story: 'What can I tell you, Miss Gladys? The tsotsies who made the cut in my body with their knife, when they tried to take my watch, did not hurt me like my wife's screaming hurt me. We took so long to get to the Hospital, and she never stopped all the way. Then, she was taken from me, my mother went with her, and I waited and waited. Then, my mother came out to me. My wife was dead. The baby, it was a boy, was dead. Gone, Miss Gladys. Dead! So then, I came back to work, and I was very different. Yes. Now, I remembered how you and your family loved one another, how you sang and laughed together. I remembered how you taught me about God, Miss Gladys, how you wrote your book to teach people how to be good. I read my Bible every day. I go to Church. I pray. I try to lead a good life, Miss Gladys. You see, I have never forgotten how you used to take time to teach me, to explain not to hurt animals. You even saved a mouse, once.'

'Yes, Tatti, I remember. It was the one Sita caught. You helped me hide it in the garden.'

We smiled at one another, picturing the scene.

I asked: 'Tatti, and how is your mother?'

'She is very old now. She talks no more of marriage to me, because she knows I will never marry again.'

When we parted, I kissed Tatti on both cheeks. His smile was radiant. I feel privileged to have known him.

There are very vulnerable people in this world.

I vividly recall a special person who came to my house one day, holding an enormous book under one arm. It was the Encyclopaedia Biblica, and had been given to him by an old man who was moving house.

I offered my visitor, tea and biscuits, whilst I inspected the item for sale. To his delight, I purchased it off him.

He had barely left the premises, when he returned: 'A very strange thing has happened,' said this priest from the Omega Church, pursing his lips, and eyeing me with a gaze akin to awe: 'I was riding my bicycle down the road, when I heard a voice say: " "You must return to this lady, for she has wisdom.".". And so, I am back, Mrs...... I have come to learn.'

Taken aback by such an utterance, I could do naught else but proffer fresh tea and another batch of cookies, to the little African, whose slight figure and prominent cheekbones reminded me of a mantis, an insect I dearly love.

This was the beginning of what was to prove a long friendship, for Father Joseph visited me regularly, asking my advice on the Sermons he was intending to deliver to his flock. He was pure in heart, a rare being.

Whenever he came, he made short thrift of my biscuit stock, which I did not mind in the least. He spoke with great deliberation, as though tasting his words before uttering them, gaze turned inwards, reading from a secret script. He had small, round eyes, hidden in folds of overhanging flesh, but they were bright and innocent. His smile was genuine, his expression as trusting as a child's. As for his conversation, he never ceased to amaze me.

'You know, Mrs......there is much ignorance. It is like a woman, who has been told that a very important visitor is coming. Well, she takes her duster, and off she goes, cleaning so much that the dust rises in the air. Then, she sees a spider – up there, in the corner of the ceiling. She takes a chair, tries to knock that spider off the wall, but it rushes to another place – now, while she is being so busy – her visitor stands at the door and knocks. Does she hear him? No, she is too busy chasing that spider. And so, her visitor goes away. Now, she stops her cleaning, sits down, and waits. No use! Let me tell you what this story means. The visitor is Jesus Christ, our Saviour. The ignorant soul is the one who thinks she can rid herself of her faults by her own efforts. The spider is the one fault she really wants to be rid of. Well, all this effort for nothing. So busy thinking she can do everything by herself, she misses the Visitor altogether. The wise soul says: 'Lord, I can do no soul - cleansing on my own. I will be very still and open my door, so that You can enter whenever You please. I know that as You enter my soul, I will be purified.'

His eyes shone, smile flashed, awaiting my reaction.

'Father Joseph, that is a modern parable. It is very good.'

Pleasure mantled his features: 'People can understand the Gospel message better in this way, you see. But there are some very ignorant souls in this world, for sure. Last week, I was riding through town, when this man shouts: "Hey there, you, priest, what are you doing, telling people about God? What God? You tell them lies, that's what you are doing." He came right up to me, running alongside, still shouting at me. Well, I stopped my bicycle, got off and said to him: "There are tsotsies (bandits), who kill people with knives and guns, but what you do, is worse. You want to kill people's souls. Be off with you. My job is to save souls." When I said this to him, the man just walked away. Yes, there are very ignorant souls in this world.'

Father Joseph reached out with delicate fingers. They hovered over the plate of goodies, then, selected a few. I watched him, amused and happy, to have him grace my table. I held him in high regard.

Out of the blue one day, his wife phoned me. Desperation coated every word: 'Mrs…it is Father Joseph's wife. We are in trouble. My husband took some tinned food from a Supermarket, and has been arrested. They are going to send him to a farm to-morrow. He will be sold.'

'Sold?' I exclaimed, horrified, 'what do you mean, Mrs Joseph?'

I heard her sobbing, then she said: 'As a prisoner, he is sold to the farmers for farm labour. The hard work will kill him, Mrs…They are taking him away in the morning. There is a bail of seventy Rands, that is why I am phoning you. My husband is a good man, but we have six children and so he was tempted.' A pause, 'I know what he did was wrong, but I am so worried about him working in the fields. Can you help us, please?' She then asked me to contact another lady to tell her of Father Joseph's plight.

I reassured her, obtained details from her where I was to bring the bail money, then, telephoned the lady as requested. She lived in the wealthy suburb of Houghton. I told her what had happened.

'Well, he need not come here again,' this lady (whom I had never met) told me, 'what a disgrace. A priest caught stealing! What next? I hope he spends a long time in jail.'

Her reaction sparked instant fire within me: 'That is a very unchristian attitude,' I said, 'Father Joseph, like each and everyone of us, gave in to a temptation, that does not make him a pariah. I shall advise him never to set foot at your place again when I next see him, because your lack of charity classifies you as a bigot, and Father Joseph should associate only with people who, like him, are tolerant and kind. Good-day to you, Madam.'

With that, I put an end to the conversation.

Next morning, at the crack of dawn, I was at our meeting-place, where a surprise awaited me. Father Joseph stood on the sidewalk beside his wife.

I expressed my joy by jumping out of the car, and pumping Father Joseph's hand energetically. His face was wreathed in smiles: 'Thank you for coming, Mrs…a true miracle has happened. A person from The Prisoner's Friend Society, paid my Bail, and here I am. I am free – no charges – I am very fortunate. Even after what I did, the Holy One looks after me.'

Tears misted his eyes. I placed an arm about him: 'Come on, into the car, both of you. I am taking you home.'

Delight on their faces, the couple obeyed. Following their directions, I drove them to their tiny house at Alexandra Township, then I spoke to Father Joseph: 'I telephoned Mrs..as you had asked. Do not go back to her, dear friend. She was very critical of you. You are too wise to allow excessive remorse to eat away at your heart. Yes, you should not have taken those tins of food, it was wrong. But we all make mistakes. Who knows, perhaps this happened to give you a lesson in humility, so that you do not become puffed up with pride.'

Father Joseph looked intently into my face: 'Could it be so, Mrs...?'

'From my experience, I have learnt it to be the case. Sometimes, like a thief who steals into your home undetected, pride enters the soul, and we are unaware of its presence, then, God allows us to fall hard...suddenly we wake up, realize what is happening, and chase the thief away.'

I took his hands in mine, even as his wife watched with tender look: 'Father Joseph, you are dearer to me now, because you have suffered this setback. You must visit me as soon as you can.'

I drove away, seeing their bright faces in my rear window, their hands waving.

We bought Father Joseph a new bicycle for Christmas, and then, life took me away from Johannesburg. I shall always remember the forlorn look on Father Joseph's face as I said good-bye.

*   *   *

My parents bought Hotel du Palais, a one-Star Hotel in the town of Montpellier in the south of France. It was situated close to the lovely Jardins du Peyroud, where brilliant blooms were laid out in artful manner, and trees afforded pleasant shade from the fierce sunlight.

Adjoining the Jardins, was an Arboretum, where the Tree-lover could discover treasures indeed amongst the rare specimens which had been brought from all over the globe.

I worked with my parents in the Hotel.

One day, a large man filled the doorway leading to the Reception area, causing me to look up from my desk.

He was accompanied by two beautiful Alsatians, who promptly sat down just inside the foyer, ears pricked to attention, tongues hanging out, as they panted in the heat.

'Have you a room for me and my dogs?' the man asked, in a deep baritone, 'it will be for three days only.'

'Of course,' I replied.

He regarded me steadily: 'You surprise me. Other Hotels will not have me. They will not admit my dogs, and I will not be separated from them.' He smiled: 'I am glad you have a room for us. I assure you my dogs are well-behaved.'

'That, I can see, Monsieur. They are superb, but they look very thirsty. May I give them some water?'

I was already on my way to the kitchen when I heard the answer: 'Yes, thank you.'

I placed water before the Alsatians, and stood back. They made no move, until their master told them: 'You may drink.'

Immediately, the pair slaked their thirst.

The man gave me a smile as broad as his shoulders: 'An animal-lover. This is my lucky day!'

Returning his smile, I took a key from the inner office, showed our guest to his room, then returned to my duties behind the Reception desk.

Later, this striking person talked to me; 'You have been very kind, Mademoiselle (very courteous to call me thus), and so, I will tell you a little about this person you have allowed into your Hotel. I was once a lawyer with a lucrative career ahead of me. I come from what is called a good family – wealthy, successful, well-established in the community. Then, one day, the thought came to me that I was surrounded by hypocrisy, by what is false…it became crystal clear to me that I must abandon such a life, and so, I left it all behind me. I am now a philosopher with no fixed abode. My best friends are my dogs. They never deceive me, will never betray me.'

I told him: 'Axel Munthe, a doctor, and a philosopher like yourself, wrote that the dog is a Saint.'

Sounding a booming laugh, our guest said: 'Exactly! In the animal, one finds truth – there is no deceit there.

I was fascinated by this larger-than-life Philosopher. Well over six feet tall, he had massive shoulders and a handsome, leonine head. His eyes shone with intelligence. Joie-de-vivre exuded from every pore. His magnetism filled the room as soon as he made an appearance. The night before his departure from our Hotel, he invited a Magistrate to cross the road for a drink. When the other hesitated, the Philosopher boomed; 'What's wrong? Do you not want to be seen drinking with me?'

I will always see the pair, as they moved away, the towering Philosopher draped in a cape (even in the hot weather), with a friendly arm about the frail shoulders of the Magistrate. Beside them strode the beautiful Alsatians, wearing expensive collars, for, as their master had told me: 'only the best, for my friends.'

It was at Montpellier, that I found Ramana. I was returning from the town-centre, when I heard terrified mewling. I turned into an alley to investigate, bumping as I did so, into a lad of about ten years old, who was holding a kitten in his arms. To be more exact, he was trying to extricate its claws from his shirt, but it clung to him in a frenzied effort to survive, instinctively aware that the open dustbin nearby, was a death-trap.

'What are you doing?' I shouted.

The boy glared at me, then continued to disengage the claws.

'I am asking you to tell me what you are going to do with that kitten? Answer me right now!'

'It's none of your business.'

'Oh yes, it is. Cruelty to animals, is my business. The gendarmes are nearby. I will fetch them here this minute.'

At my threat, the lad changed his tune: 'My mother told me to get rid of it. She told me to put it in the dustbin.'

'Well, you just give me that kitten. You can tell your mother I have taken it from you. It is a disgrace – such wickedness! How dare you treat an animal in this way!'

With that, I took the tan- and- black kitten into my arms, gave the sullen boy a withering look, then made my way home.

As soon as I held the shivering mite to my heart, she ceased struggling, made no further sound, even as I spoke to her in special tones intended to soothe and console. Ramana had entered my life. I have often been told that this sensitivity I possess, is a thing I should attempt to rid myself of, that, I make a rod form my own back, etc. There is not need to make reply to such utterances, for I know that to 'Dare to do right – Dare to be true' entails assuming responsibility, making commitments…God needs warriors, not weaklings. To be gentle, merciful, compassionate, is to be truly strong. To give of oneself entails integrity of spirit, bypassing the criticism, the opinion of others. With humans, such commitment is rendered difficult because there is always the possibility of rejection. One cannot force human beings to love you, but animals are so pure, that they welcome overtures of sincere love.

Ramana grew to become a very lovely cat-lady, playing games with my father, by peeping at him from under the curtains, then suddenly pouncing on his feet. Often, she would perch on wardrobes, watching her human family from her high vantage points.

When I returned to South Africa, a Belgian lady who was a Cat-minder, took Ramana into her already very full Cat-Hotel, which I had visited. I was satisfied that this kindly soul would love Ramana, and so I left her in good hands.

Returning to Zig and Zag, our lives flowed on. I studied books on herbs, fascinated by the curative abilities of plants I had hitherto never even heard of. Now, I left the nettles where they were, in my flower beds, trimming only dense patches, for I had learnt how necessary they were, to the richness, the vigour of the soil. I poured infusions of nettles over my pot plants, marvelling at how quickly they reacted to the nettle tonic. After shampoos, I rinsed my hair with cooled infusions of this wonderful herb, pleased at their shine.

The famous French healer, Maurice Messegé, wrote that one could treat Rheumatism by placing a leaf of cabbage, still hot from having been ironed, over the painful area, leave it awhile, then repeat the process. At the time, two of my knuckles were swollen and painful. I had showed them to the doctor, but the pills prescribed had had no effect whatsoever. I decided to follow the instructions of Maurice Messegué. I took a piece of raw cabbage, ironed it, wound it round each knuckle, bound it with an elastic, waited a few minutes, unwound the by-now cold cabbage piece, ironed it, wound it about the finger…for about ten minutes. I did this, thrice a day. Three days later, my knuckles were normal. Needless to say, I was delighted. Following Messegués further advice, I tried boiling lettuce for a few minutes, then drinking the water to induce sleep. It proved to be very relaxing indeed. 5

My study of Herbs, made me an enthusiastic mouthpiece. If something is wonderful, why not spread the good news? When visiting my sister in Johannesburg, I amused my family by drinking only Herbal teas, inviting my sister to sample some also.

I still continued writing articles on the inner life for 'The Mountain Path', a spiritual Journal, published by the Ashram of the Sage, Sri Ramana Maharshi, in the South of India. I had also written a children's book on 'The Little People'. Zig and Zag had grown to adulthood, worked out a routine for themselves as they wandered off to gaze at the mild-eyed cows, and their enchanting calves. We had seen foxes loping across the emerald grasses, quickly disappearing from sight, as farmers were certainly not their allies! Badgers were often found dead on the roads, the tragic consequence of their inexperience with speeding traffic. Sometimes on my walks, I would see tiny hedgehogs who had also fallen victim to modern vehicles, lying like discarded toys, on the road.

And then, a ginger and cream Tom peeped at us from a thicket. When he warily emerged, he proved to be very thin, his coat lustreless. His eyes however, were very bright, shining with the will to survive.

I placed some food and drink in the shed for him, watching from a distance as he ate ravenously. Zig and Zag observed him also, utterly fascinated.

It was the beginning of a beautiful friendship. Hadji would suddenly disappear for days at a time, only to return coated with blood, evidence of battles between males for the attentions of the 'femmes fatales.' Armed with the antibiotic cream I had obtained from our Vet, I approached Hadji with determined step, picked him up, and proceeded to put the ointment on his wounds. The clear, green eyes stared into my face, ears waving about like delicate antennae as I chided him: 'Do you think it is worth it? Look at this mess! And all over a lady. You are crazy! Still, it is no use talking to you men – you never listen!'

Hadji was as good as gold. For a wild cat, he was very gentle, allowing me to clean his wounds, put salve on them, then take him in my arms and cradle him. Soon, he used to come looking for his daily cuddle which I call 'Gaté, Gaté'. (French equivalent to being spoilt).

Often, I would dance with him in my arms, singing to him the while. Hadji would close his eyes in contented repose.

One day, our battle-scarred warrior fell in love. He showed her off to us. She was very lovely, very petite, with the tiniest white, grey visage, dominated by slanting eyes of clear green. Her movements were of porcelain. She possessed a fragile delicacy, which bordered on watching a ballet performed upon a cloud, when she moved.

We named her, Moonflower.

Their love-story is a touching one. It is not often one sees such selfless and utter devotion. Hadji sheltered his sweetheart from biting winds, by placing her against the hedges, whilst his body took the brunt of the blasts. He waited for her to eat first. It was she who sampled the warm milk, before he took a sip. They were inseparable, walking side by side along the road or across the fields, two pilgrims sharing a splendid adventure.

Hadji came to me, asking me to approve of his wild Moonflower, who had been treated very harshly by humans at some time in her life, for she shied away from us, eyes aflame with distrust, body stiff with apprehension. Aware of her intense disquiet, we let her be, allowing her the space she required.

Zig had had enough! These invaders of her territory were trying her patience. She would tolerate it no longer. Her steady gaze never left Moonflower, but caution warned Zig not to attack whilst Hadji was around, for he was very strong. So, Zig contented herself with low growls, a twitching of the tail, menacing signals she served on Moonflower: 'If I catch you, my girl, watch it!'

The delicate beauty heeded the warning, never coming near, if Hadji was not with her.

One morning, a black and white female startled us, by accompanying the sweethearts to their breakfast. She was emaciated, had the same haunted look about her as Black Mist had worn in London. She cried piteously for mercy. She found it.

Gentleman that he was, Hadji allowed Lotus Blossom as we named her, to eat first. I hurried to fill another dish.

Soon, the trio were at the food, Lotus Blossom quivering with pleasure and relief.

From the kitchen window, Zig growled furiously, this newest invasion would be dealt with as soon as the male was off with his lady. What was this world coming to? Accordingly, when Hadji and Moonflower moved down the fields, Zig launched herself through the air, chasing Lotus Blossom down the garden path. A triumphant Zig came back, with slow, majestic pace 'That's that!' written all over her face.

Lotus Blossom appeared henceforth only when Hadji was there. Longing for affection, she tried to insinuate herself into the house, but Zig, ferret-like, searched indefatigably for the intruder, deep growls issuing from her throat. They alerted me to what was going on, so that I was able to save Lotus Blossom from unpleasant encounters. Life is not smooth!

Walking in the fields one day, I saw some horses being led to lush pastures. They suddenly reminded me of a time in my youth.

We had been living in a beautiful, old-fashioned farmhouse, complete with a circular veranda, five picturesque Rondavels, a tennis court, cowshed, vegetable and flower gardens. We played host to many guests. One of them a young man of about twenty five years, thin and earnest-faced, stated one mealtime, that women were not as daring as men.

As a sixteen-year-old-female, I told him he spoke nonsense. Our neighbour's daughter was present. The male chauvinist asked her is she would loan us one of her horses. When she answered in the affirmative, he turned to me: 'You say women are equal in adventurous spirit to me. All right then, I challenge you to ride a horse for the first time, with all of us as witnesses. I say you will be thrown off like a shot!'

I stood up, my arms in the air:' Of course I will ride Paddy's horse. Nothing to it, and I will not fall off, I promise you. What makes you think men are so superior, anyway?'

Maman and papa were not happy about this foolhardy venture looming on the horizon, voicing their fears in no uncertain terms, but my ire was up, womanhood required a champion, and I would not flinch from being a female knight…they resigned themselves to the inevitable – when their eldest child was in this mood, there was no retraining her.

At three p.m., clad in shorts (folly), I was helped on to a horse, whom Paddy had assured me, was mild-natured. Once seated, I realized it was a long way to the ground. My paternal grandmother was already fingering her Rosary beads, papa and maman tried to look unconcerned, the male chauvinist had a smile on his face, anticipating disaster. The other members of the family who had come to spend the week-end, and some friends, cheered me as my horse began to move away. I had absolutely no idea what to do with the reins I held in my hands. Paddy had given me the scantiest instructions on horse-riding, so that what had appeared to be straightforward and easy to understand, now became a blur, as my body was bounced up and down by the trotting of the animal whose power I began to feel in no uncertain manner, when he suddenly decided to gallop.

'Hang on like a sack of mealies!' shouted Paddy, as the horse stormed down the driveway, on to the road, then swerved to the left, tearing along the sand-track between our farms.

How does a sack of mealies hang on? Came the thought, as I hugged the animal with my knees and rested my chest against the arched, muscular neck, Come what may, I would cling to the mane if necessary, but, I would not be parted from this flying creature who was shaking every bone of my body loose from their moorings.

Now, I definitely heard how loudly the wind can whistle. My eyes were wet from the force of air rushing past me like a thousand arrows. There was no time to think about Paddy's instructions, only the grim battle to stay in the saddle dominated my being, forcing me to pay close attention to what this 'mild-mannered' creature intended for me. I was not kept in the dark for long! He decided he had had enough of this inexperienced greenhorn, and wanted me off his back, so he galloped closer to' The barbed wire on the righthand-side of the track.

Unfortunately for him, I detected this ploy in time to raise my right leg, yanking the reins reflexively to the left. The horse responded, leaving the ugly wire, and staying in the middle of the track. I was not feeling too good by this time, gritting my teeth at the chafing on the skin of my thighs. What had possessed me to wear shorts? The heat!

My ears were filled with thunder, with strange, rushing sounds, my eyes stung, my posterior was on fire, as were my thighs…this being a female Knight, was certainly not for the faint-hearted.

And now, the horse decided to go back the way we had come. I hung on grimly, determined that the 'man' would not win the wager. Come what may, I would climb out of this saddle on my own. Up and down I went, my fingers clutching the reins fiercely, eyes still watering, hair flying in the wind. I silently resolved to be more prudent in future when accepting a duel.

Suddenly, it was over. The horse stopped where we had met, and not a moment too soon, as far as I was concerned. I stifled my groans, forced a smile on my face as I crawled out of the saddle, to deafening cheers.

The 'man' stared at me, admiration written all over his face: 'That was great!' he said, 'I must try it also. Will you come with me to-morrow? We can go to the Lido Hotel – they have horses there.'

I groaned inwardly: 'Why not?' I answered.

The next day, I accompanied my converted Chauvinist to where two horses awaited us. I mounted, Phillip did likewise. Our ride had begun. Little did we know how it would end.

For a while, all was well, then, I saw danger. Phillip had his eyes on a low branch a short distance away, but what he had not noticed, was the sharp edge of a pigsty roof, jutting out to his left. Even as I shouted a warning, the corrugated iron sliced his leg from knee to ankle. He gave a strangled scream, looked down, reached for the wounded area.

'Jump!' I called out.

Phillip threw himself from the saddle, rolling on the grass in anguish, face ashen, pain causing him to double up.

By this time I was at his side, where I immediately saw the extent of his injury. To stop him thrashing about, I sat astride his chest, pinning his arms to the ground, whilst I shouted to my sister: 'Jackie! Get the Manager, quick!'

By now, Phillip had almost lost consciousness. His eyes had become glassy, his breathing ugly, a gasping, tearing sound. I did not know how much blood he had lost.

Suddenly, there was a flurry of activity to my left. I caught sight of men running towards us. The Manager raised me up, Phillip was carried to a car, into which my sister and I were hastily bundled, then, it shot off for Johannesburg's Hospital in Hillbrow.

It was a nightmare journey, with Phillip's head resting on my lap, his eyes staring at me, naked with fear, silently asking for reassurance. I did the best I could, but tears slid down my cheeks as I saw his blood on my clothes, on my hands, perhaps even on my face, for I had had no time to tidy myself up.

At last he was whisked away from us, and wheeled into the Emergency area. Jackie and I frightened the wits out of our maman when we entered her Hotel, blood-bespattered, weeping, and accompanied by the Manager of the Lido Hotel. He related the events of the past few hours to her.

Maman held us close, murmuring words of comfort. She was very distressed, losing no time in alerting the family, normal procedure in times of crises.

Soon, we were huddled together, sharing the experiences of so many humans all over the world who pace along corridors, drink endless cups of tea or coffee, talking in hushed voices, eyes aching as they stare at the doors from whence those all-important doctors would emerge to bring news.

Phillip was a Notary, having arrived from Mauritius but a few weeks previously, his family known to ours. Now, he lay on his bed of pain. When we were allowed to see him, he tried to greet us with a brave smile, but his features were still ashen. He looked at me: 'So, it was I who fell from the horse! I take back all I said about the female sex. You were wonderful!'

I felt myself blushing. He licked his lips, turned his head to address the others: 'If I have learned one lesson today, it is that one should not be so daring.'

We did not stay long, afraid of tiring him. Every bone in my body ached as I sank back in the back seat of my parents' car, on the way home. It had been a nightmarish day, whirling us all along on a forced carousel ride, picking up speed, until we could hold on only with great difficulty. How foolhardy we had been, clambering into saddles full of bravado, intent on proving ourselves, yet it had been brought home to us that such stupidity had a price. Phillip was lying in hospital. I had been spattered with his blood. I felt guilty somehow, for had I not been the show-off the previous day, trying to prove how brave, how daring I could be?

I crept into my maman's arms, my favourite refuge.

Wise as always, she found the right words: 'You must not blame yourself, my bien-aimée, (beloved). It is good to dare, to be impulsive, impetuous. It is a fire with us which is a brave fire, it encourages us to try something new, something different…the timid who never attempt to do anything other than that which they know, play safe – they cannot know what it is like to be adventurous – to trust in their ability to deal with challenging situations. See how your father and I, left Madagascar, the place where you were born, to come here. We dared to face the unknown. Courage is always rewarded. What happened to Phillip is an accident, nothing more. Because you are sensitive and have imagination, you think somehow you are to blame. Put that thought out of your mind. We will visit Phillip often, soon, he will be on the mend. Dry your eyes.'

We went into the kitchen to make ourselves some hot cocoa, my favourite bed-time drink. I felt much better already.

Our patient spent many weeks in hospital, emerging with a very ugly-looking scar, still a bright-red colour. I doubt he ever rode a horse again. I did.

Apart from my adventure with the horse-family, there is a very amusing tale about hens.

Our parents had decided that the only way their children would ever improve in the second language required by the school curriculum, Afrikaans, was to live on the farm of an Afrikaans-speaking family for awhile.

Accordingly, we saw ourselves ensconced amongst Afrikaners, who had been asked to converse to us only in their mother tongue.

Oupa Pretorius, tall, thin, with a leathery skin, piercing blue eyes, and a goatee-beard, took us in hand, bringing us with him on long walks, where he often headed for the kopjes (hills). There, he would seat us on large boulders, whilst he filled his pipe, preparatory to inhaling the very strong tobacco he favoured. A few mighty puffs would see him wreathed in smoke, then, he would begin: 'Ja, children, there are strange stories to tell. The old folk did not drive fast cars, use elevators, fly in airplanes, they did not need these things to make them happy. Youngsters learned respect for their elders, spoke very politely to everyone, not like these days, where they knock against you on the town pavements without even apologising. No, things were different then. Nature taught quietly, without fuss. Here, one walked softly, the land was holy, creatures had their place, and the old folk knew how to read nature's signs. Here, a buck had crossed near the path, there, a leopard or lion had stalked its prey – over there, one could detect the print of a Hottentot or perhaps, even a Bushman…ja, in those days folk were very wise, alert, they could bake delicious bread in ovens under the ground, such fine-tasting soetkoekies, koeksusters also, with golden syrup trapped inside them. Oh, it was so lekker (nice) – magtig! I tell you, it was like eating a honeycomb.'

We loved listening to Oupa Pretorius' stories. Once, he told us: 'Children, one must always respect wild animals – not try to tame them into pets as one farmer did. He was so strong, this boer, he had a neck like a bull, boasted to all how he could tame anything. Well, one day, he got himself a lion cub, from where I do not know, but that is not important. He started training this cub like he trained his dogs. Oh, this boer had to control everyone and everything. Even his wife had to obey his orders he gave her, poor lady. Anyhow, this cub grew into a beautiful adult. People were not too pleased when this lion appeared. Magtig! Those paws he had! Still, one tried to put a brave face on it, because one knew that this farmer was watching, laughing inside because he knew this lion caused us to be fearful. Time passed. This farmer sat in his chair one afternoon, dozing after lunch. His lion licked one hand which dangled from the armrest. He licked again, because there was some blood on it where this farmer had cut himself. Well, I will not frighten you with any details, just to finish this true story I will say that the lion sprang on the farmer and killed him.'

At our horrified gasps, he nodded sagely: 'Ja, this fellow paid for his arrogance. A wild animal must be treated with respect.'

One day, papa bought some beautiful Leghorn Whites, and Rhode Island Reds (varieties of hens), from a specialised Shop in Johannesburg. He was returning to the Pretorius farm with my maternal aunt, Miriam, whom he had picked up at her work place. She was coming to spend the week-end with us.

He parked the car, in front of the Bank.

'I have to pop in, for a minute,' he told my aunt, as he got out. Off he went, nimbly climbing the steps.

After a while, my aunt opened the window, then, feeling too hot, she opened the door, stepped out on to the pavement.

Meanwhile, papa stood patiently in the long queue, which was a normal feature of Fridays.

Suddenly, something flew through the air. Startled cries. Another form appeared, this time, landing in front of an amazed Teller.

Papa blanched. Oh no! But it was indeed his precious hens, cascading like feathered waterfalls on to the Bank's customers; squawking, clucking, flying, skittering across the polished surfaces.

Papa was riveted to the floor with mortification. He wanted to vanish somewhere – anywhere!

My aunt came over to him, hat askew, eyes wide with apprehension: 'Henry, I only opened the door...'

She received an angry glare, then, papa swung into action, enlisting the help of some bemused men and women.

Even the Bank Manager lent a hand, anxious to rid the premises of such unwelcome customers.

On the marble steps, some hens who relished their new-found freedom, preened their feathers in the sunshine, totally oblivious of the passers-by who stood to gape at them.

When all the runaways had been collected, papa drove away with what appeared to be superb sangfroid. A very chastened Aunt Miriam had to undergo a severe tongue-lashing all the way to the farm, for papa was still smarting, and she had indeed been very careless.

Once, when we visited the Kruger National Park, a warden told us that he and his colleague had witnessed an amazing sight. It happened in this way. Game Rangers go on regular patrols. On one such patrol, they noticed an old cow-elephant, whose body was riddled with open sores. She appeared to be very ill. Whenever she attempted to leave the herd, they crowded lovingly around her, preventing her from leaving them, no doubt because they knew she wished to die alone, away from the herd. The wardens resolved to return the next day to put her out of her misery.

When they arrived the following morning, rifles at the ready, they beheld, to their surprise, a huge Bull-elephant charging towards the sick animal. Suddenly, he made a rapid lunge, his tusk bit deep into the cow's temple, then it was withdrawn. Without a sound, the cow-elephant fell to the ground, killed instantly.

'This was the first time we had ever witnessed Euthanasia practised amongst elephants,' this Game warden told us. 'It was an extraordinary sight. That bull-elephant drove his tusk precisely where we would have aimed a bullet.'

He then told us about two men who had got out of their vehicle when it broke down. This is strictly prohibited in the Kruger National Park. These men were tinkering under the car when, to their amazement, it rose into the air. Their astonishment turned to blind panic when they saw that it was an enormous elephant who was lifting it. Luckily for them, the elephant contented himself with rolling it over, then strolling casually off into the bush.

On another occasion, an A.A. mechanic was busy repairing a stranded motorist's vehicle, when three lionesses padded into view. Frozen with fear, the mechanic remained where he was, while the felines walked about the car under the mesmerised gaze of the motorist...after a while, the lionesses moved away.

This story was told to us by the A.A. mechanic himself. It came about in this way. We had suffered a breakdown after having just passed Pretorius Kop Gate, and I had told papa that I thought I knew what was wrong. As I tried to open the door to get out, papa, quite rightly, ordered me to stay where I was. Papa then asked a passing motorist to alert the A.A. at Skukuza Camp. When the mechanic appeared on the scene, he circled our car several times scrutinizing the ground carefully, then, he told us his story.

'I am very cautious now,' he said, 'after those lionesses, I take my time before standing out here in the open.'

Because there were no Bungalows available that night at Camp, we had perforce to sleep in the tents provided. Papa was not happy about this, but his apprehension grew when I told him that a warden I had met at the Cafeteria, had warned me: 'Papa, he told me that we must be very careful if we want to go to the Cloakroom at night, because there are hyenas who forage about in the dustbins.'

'What?' exclaimed my parent, glancing at maman, 'do you hear that, Alix?'

'I don't think we need worry,' replied maman, 'we would not be allowed to sleep in these tents if there was any danger.'

My impish spirit came to the fore: 'Well, we must shine our torches on them if we do see them, although I doubt whether that will help us much. Hyenas are not as cowardly as many people imagine!'

Papa stared at me: 'What do you mean?'

'Well, I have just been reading the book 'Man Is The Prey', and the author gives statistics. He says that there are many people killed by hyenas whilst they sleep...they have been attacked in the open,...one snap of those huge jaws over a face, and the poor victim does not stand a chance.'

Papa's eyes opened wide: 'That is not reassuring at all!'

I could not help laughing.

'What is so funny?' my papa asked, irritation creeping into his voice, 'we were quite content, until you come here with these ghastly stories about hyenas, now, I know I shall not sleep comfortably this night.'

Maman smiled: 'She is only telling us what she has read!'

Papa replied in a disgruntled voice: 'That is the trouble. She reads too much.'

I kissed them good-night before retiring to my tent, chuckling to myself over papa's reaction. I had been quite impossible!

As I pulled the blankets about me, I thought I heard a sniffling noise. Was I imagining things? There it was again. Definitely something out there. In the other bed, my son was fast asleep. My lips twitched, as I heard papa ask: 'Did you hear that, Alix – Francis?'

My mother and brother made no answer. Only papa and I were still awake.

Sleep eluded me for some time, for, is the truth be told, I had scared myself with my stories about the massive jaws breaking the bones of unsuspecting victims.

Papa had told me, how his family had once played a joke on him in Mauritius one night, whilst sojourning at the seaside on holiday. At this Campement (bungalow), there were dividing walls, which did not reach to the ceiling, thus allowing air to circulate freely in the summer.

His brothers, sister and mother, had tied strings to his bed sheets before retiring to their quarters for the night, knowing full well that papa would come to bed only in the early hours of the morning. At supper, they had steered the conversation towards the eerie, the ghostly, the supernatural, so as to 'condition' papa for what was to come. Unsuspecting, papa eventually crept into bed, taking care not to put on the light, so as not to disturb the occupants sharing the bungalow.

Moonlight lit up the area sufficiently. Once in bed, papa lay flat on his back, his hands grasping the sheets firmly. Sleep usually claimed him like a babe, not this night, however. Just as he dozed off, papa felt a tug. His eyes flew open, there, another one! Gently, papa pulled the sheets back under his chin, but to no avail, inexorably, they slid down further and further till they reached his knees, then, suddenly, there was a vertical take-off as the sheets rose high in the air. Papa was out of the bed, out of the room, out of the house…laughter floated on the air. The culprits appeared, among them his mother, tears pouring down her cheeks, the handkerchief she had stuffed into her mouth to stifle her merriment, still clutched in one hand.

Papa looked sheepish, then, he joined in the peals of laughter.

Another story papa recounted, took place when his mother was pregnant with him.

Prior to his marriage to my grandmother, my grandfather, Lewis Rawstorne, had always had Masses celebrated for the Holy Souls in Purgatory. With the wedding preparations, the arrival of his bride on the property, the months passed by so swiftly, that grandpère Lewis had forgotten about the Holy Masses.

One night, as he and his wife were partaking of supper, a fearful din broke out from the direction of the kitchen. Pots, pans, crockery, appeared to be dancing, smashing, dashing about…grandmére uttered cries of alarm. Her husband rushed to investigate. Terrified servants had bolted from the premises into the garden, where they were discovered, shivering and exploding into high-pitched wailing. Grandpére silenced them with his calm demeanour, then, he examined the kitchen carefully. Everything appeared to be in order. Nothing had been displaced or broken. It took some time to restore a modicum of peace, to the still-jittery staff, but soon the household was ready to retire.

As the couple proceeded up the staircase, their candles were blown out. Grandmère cried out. Grandpère told her that there was nothing to be alarmed about. He re-lit the candles, again they were blown out. Grandpére guided his wife along, until they reached the sanctuary of their bedroom. There, he lit the lamp. Soon, they were settled in bed. Footsteps, loud and rapid, were heard on the landing. Grandmère sat up, stifling a cry. The door resounded to an urgent knocking, then, it flew open. Grandpère got quietly out of bed, padded across to the door, closed it. He soothed his frightened wife: 'Ma chère, everything has an explanation. Do not be distressed.'

During the days that followed, things got worse. Bedclothes were removed from the bed, the noises grew louder, on the highly-polished surface of the dining-room table manifested a thick layer of fine dust, the mysterious nature of which, caused grandpère to leap on to the thick wooden beams decorating the ceiling, to investigate a possible human presence. There was nothing to be seen.

Grandpère told a maid to polish the table. She did so. No sooner had the curious dust been removed, that it reappeared, this time, even thicker than before.

My grandfather took his wife to her parents' home until an explanation could be found to explain the phenomena manifesting on their own property. His brother-in-law laughed at his sister's nervous state.

'Mon ami,' said Grandpère amiably, 'why do you not come back with me, seeing you are so bold and brave.'

The two men returned to Plains Wilhems, the Sugar Cane Plantation where Grandpére was Administrator.

When the disturbances began, grandpére carried on eating. His visitor was decidedly uneasy.

By 2 a.m. the young man had had enough. Still clad in his sleeping-garments, he made off for the sanctuary of his home.

As for my grandfather, he possessed nerves of steel. He lived in the residence for several weeks on his own. Then, it occurred to him that he had omitted having Masses said for the Dead. Chiding himself for having been so remiss, he went to see the priest to ask for the Masses to be resumed.

The manifestations stopped. Grandmère returned to her home.

Papa always ended this story with: 'And then, people ask why I have a nervous temperament? Do you wonder?'

In fact, as I knew full well, my papa was a very brave man. Maman told me how he had once saved the life of a woman in Madagascar, when he had traversed swollen rivers infested with crocodiles, and dense forests, to fetch a doctor for the lady who was in labour. She would have died in childbirth, if it had not been for that daring and courageous drive on pap's motorbike. The doctor had been very unwilling to come, but papa had dragged him out of his comfortable home, brooking no argument. The terrified medic had clung for dear life on to papa's waist, as they tore along. The champagne downed afterwards, had revived the doctor and put the smiles back on his face.

Lying in my tent in the Kruger Park, I chuckled as I visualized the stories which papa had told us about his youth, and the pranks which had been played on him.

Maman gave us all a terrible fright, when we stopped at the Tea Kiosk the next day. It was one of the spots where people may leave their cars. As we drank tea, and ate delicious scones, gorgeous starlings strutted about the tables, bright eyes darting hither and thither, intent on discovering titbits. Maman spied a huge elephant feeding nearby. She advanced towards it, hand outstretched, thinking that this elephant was tame because of its proximity to the Cafeteria.

We screamed a warning, absolutely terrified for her.

The magnificent bull-elephant turned his head. Our screams reached maman's ears. She ran.

Papa herded us all into the car.

'What did you think you were doing?' he asked his wife, visibly shaken by her narrow escape.

Maman's lovely eyes widened: 'It looked so peaceful, munching away at the leaves. I wanted to stroke its trunk, as we do in the Zoo in Johannesburg.'

Papa looked at her with incredulous gaze: 'But, we are in the Kruger Park, not the Zoo!'

Suddenly, he saw the comical side of it. Maman, lulled into a false sense of security, advancing towards a wild bull-elephant, holding a fruit in one hand. He burst out laughing, shaking his head. We joined in.

Papa kept a close watch on maman from that moment on, fearing her intrepid spirit could land her into another potentially dangerous situation.

Elephants can be very terrifying.

Three years ago, on a visit to the Kruger Park, I was a passenger with my nephew, Jean-Pierre and Jackie, my sister. Her husband, Jan, drove the Combi along a track of road. We spied an elephant some distance away.

'Stop, Jan,' said my sister.

'He will move away,' replied my brother-in-law, his foot exerting pressure on the accelerator.

I leaned forward in my seat, becoming nervous.

It was no doubt contagious, for both Jean-Pierre and Jackie, did likewise.

'Jan, don't go on,' my sister urged.

By this time, we were quite near to the massive creature, who was quietly feeding near the side of the track.

I was filled with disquiet.

'If it decides to come down this road, there is no place for it to go past,' was my contribution.

My prophetic words proved accurate, for, at that moment the elephant turned, heading straight for us.

'Jan, reverse! Reverse!' sounded his wife.

'Hurry! Quick!, shouted Jean-Pierre.

'Don't panic,' Jan said, sending us careering backwards at the same time. The elephant come on.

Jan stalled the engine.

I joined the chorus of: 'Hurry, let us get out of here!'. My heart was in my throat at sight of this huge animal heading straight for us.

Jan started the engine, and we continued going in reverse, whilst the elephant moved his ears in irritation at our presence and the noise we were making. It decided to increase its speed.

For some unaccountable reason, my brother-in-law chose that moment to turn the Combi in that narrow space. To our terror, we stalled again.

By this time, his three passengers were standing, shrieking with fright. I was not ashamed to sound my alarm in this fashion.

'What are you doing?' Jackie asked her husband, her eyes fixed on the elephant closing in on us.

'Jan!' I cried, 'he is going to ram us, for sure!'

'Help!' shouted Jean-Pierre.

A few deft gear-changes, the Combi miraculously moved speedily out of danger. Behind us, the angry elephant was pounding along, intent on seeing off these intruders.

To our relief we came on to a main road. We drove off.

A few hours later, a motorist leaned out of his window to tell us: 'Be careful when you come to that track road near Skukuza. There is a huge elephant there, who must be avoided. He is very bad-tempered.'

We knew all about that.

Our morning encounter so unnerved us, that at midday when a grasshopper landed on my sister's throat, she screamed. Jan stopped the Combi, she leaped out, flapping her arms. In sympathy, I also shrieked, opened the door on my side, and jumped on to the road. My poor brother-in-law just stared!

And as though that was not enough, whilst we were enjoying the view at a look-out point, a troop of baboons swooped from the trees, sending us running for the Combi, sounding loud cries of alarm.

On the eve of our arrival at the Game Reserve, there had been a terrible tragedy, when a warden who had accompanied tourists on a Night Tour of the Park, had walked along a bridge to make sure the area was safe. He had been attacked and killed by a leopard who had been crouching in the undergrowth nearby.

We have often seen people standing beside their cars, flagrantly disobeying the rules. On one occasion, we had sighted two leopards where only a few moments later, a tourist stood to take a photograph. We told her about the leopards. She quickly entered her vehicle.

As Oupa Pretorius had said: 'Wild animals must be treated with respect.'

*   *   *

PROWLER

======

Our nearest neighbour was a bachelor in his sixties, who had lived in the parental bungalow all his life. He was rather a hermit, tending his vegetable plot, caring for the few cattle he had, an old donkey called Brandy, and was always to be seen shadowed by his black and white Collie, Prowler.

This neighbour fell ill with advanced cancer, was suddenly whisked off to hospital one day, where he remained for a month. Whilst he was away, I fed Prowler, who, unused to strangers intruding on his master's property, growled at my approach. I spoke to him soothingly as I put down food for him, walking with purposeful steps to the outside tap, where I filled his water dish, aware of the warnings he gave me, as I did so.

When the patient returned, we paid him a visit to enquire after his health, and ask whether there was anything we could do for him. He gave us a shy grin: 'Thanks, missus, for feeding Prowler. Now, he is not so sure he wants to go back to my cooking!'

We laughed together, looking at the Collie at his side.

'I would be glad to have some apples – the sweet, red ones, for my canary,' Jimmy told us, his thin face ravaged by the illness coursing through him. We asked him over for a meal, and he entertained us with yarns about rural folk he had known throughout the years.

We brought him the apples his canary found delicious, and I often walked down the road with an extra apple pie on Baking days, handing it over to our neighbour in an effort to whet his appetite.

Some months later, we attended his funeral. When the cortège halted for a few minutes outside his home, we saw Prowler standing guard at the front door, head turned enquiringly at the long line of cars near the property. He did not stir from his post.

It grew bitterly cold, and I worried about Prowler sleeping on the cold, cement floor of the shed, excluded from the warm hearth he used to share with his master. We had tried coaxing the collie to our place, but he refused to leave his master's land, taking up his position across the threshold, head on his paws, eyes, mirrors of sadness.

I brought down an old carpet, a blanket, some dishes, in which to put his food and bones I cooked in the oven for him. Prowler continued to growl when I appeared, but he ceased baring his teeth at me, which was a good sign. A woman passed by on a bicycle one day. 'He will eat you!' she warned. I smiled at her, but made no reply. The dog had to be fed, it was as simple as that!

Snow fell. Prowler slept on his carpet and the blanket I had placed there for him. He watched as I came down the road, still suspicious, but, after a few weeks, he stopped growling altogether. My husband helped me. Using his walking stick, Vincent walked carefully along the snow-covered road, carrying Prowler's food-dish in a carrier bag. He too, spoke in quiet tones to the collie, who gradually learned to accept this stranger as well.

One day I saw Prowler out on the road, on the look-out for me. As I drew closer, his tail began to wag, then, he put up his head expectantly, as though saying: 'You can pat me now. I trust you.'

Overjoyed, I stroked his fine head, realizing how difficult it must have been for Prowler to have surrendered his fierceness, and overcome his distrust of strangers.

From that day on, the collie greeted my husband and myself, with an enthusiasm which in time, deepened into affection, as he ran to meet us at meal-times.

I used to place his cooked bones on a foil-plate. To our amusement one morning, we saw him take bones and plate in his mouth, heading for nearby fields where, having followed him at a discreet distance, we saw him put the plate down, scoop the earth away with strong, energetic paws, after which he buried his treasures, returning with a decidedly muddy nose.

To my dismay one day, I found Prowler bleeding from a deep gash in the neck. He lay on his blanket with a feverish glitter in his eyes, watching me without lifting his head, confirming my fears that he was very much under the weather. Fetching fresh water, I placed it beside him, deciding I would return with an antibiotic that afternoon, but my husband advised me to wait until the next day: 'He is very strong. Give him twenty-four hours. I am sure his recuperative powers are such that he will be on his feet by the morning.'

He was right. The next day I saw the familiar black and white figure standing in the road on stiff legs, head turned towards our property, tail beating the air. Prowler came to meet me.

And now, fifteen months had passed since his master's death, and still Prowler kept vigil, eyes peering for that beloved figure he had not seen for such a long time.

Autumn was upon us. As I threw the bread on to the ground for the birds, a Robin came to inspect me. He knew me well. The clever little fellow, so small, yet so brave, stared at me as I sat caressing Prowler's handsome head.

My heart was heavy, tear-clouds gathered in my inner skies. I was waiting for the Vet.

It was so very peaceful I looked at Prowler: 'It is time to say good-bye, dearest friend, faithful heart, so loyal, so true! I have had to make this decision, to end your earthly cycle, for you are so ill…I cannot stand by, and see you labouring for breath as you are doing now. I have learnt to love you, Prowler. Go with God, little one, you will soon suffer no more!'

The Robin stood on the cold ground, head cocked to one side, as though aware of what was happening.

I heard the Vet approach. Soon, Prowler's heart bet no more. I closed the shed-door. Burial would take place only thirty-six hours later.

My husband accompanied me when it was time. We placed the body in one of my sheets, wrapped the fine head in one of my sweaters, carried him to the grave, where I placed some holy statues, which had belonged to Prowler's master. Across Prowler's heart-place, I draped a Rosary.

I returned the next day with some plants, which I arranged on Prowler's grave. The words of Axel Munthe, in his wonderful life-story, 'The Story of San Michele' came to mind as I did so: 'On the whole, it is easy to understand the dog and learn to read his thoughts. The dog cannot dissimulate, cannot deceive, cannot lie…The dog is a saint. He is straightforward and honest by nature. He looks upon his master as his king, almost as his god. He expects his god to be severe if need by, but he expects him to be just. He knows that his god can read his thoughts, and he knows it is no good to conceal them…when his king is sad and worried he knows that his time has come, and he creeps up and lays his head on his lap. "Don't worry. Never mind if they all abandon you. Let us go for a walk and forget all about it."'

Sometimes I came there to stand under the towering trees, gazing out over the fields, my feet touching the soil where a beautiful Dog-person's mortal frame had been laid to rest. It was fitting that he had been buried where his heart was. I knew that on another dimension, Prowler and his master walked together again, joy in every step, for how can love's bond ever be broken?

'Dear Lord! If You should grant me by Your Grace
To see You face to face in heaven, O then
Grant that a poor dog look into the face
Of him who was as god among men!

(Francis Jammes)

*   *   *

Meanwhile, Hadji and Moonflower's love-story continued to amaze and delight us. It became apparent she was heavily pregnant, seeing which, I prepared a warm 'house' for her, hoping it would entice her inside, when her confinement was upon her, for she refused point-blank to allow us to come close.

When I opened the front door one morning, a cry of surprise escaped me. My husband hurried to my side. There, before us, was a new-born kitten, squirming on the doormat. At ground level sat the parents, pride in their offspring written all over them.

'How wonderful!' I said, 'clever Moonflower. Clever Hadji.'

If anyone tells me that animals do not smile, I will simply look at such a person with pity, for Moonflower and Hadji definitely beamed.

Then, in swift movement, Moonflower bounded to her kitten's side, picked it up, and proceeded to walk back to the turf-shed-house with it firmly grasped in her mouth, totally disregarding its outraged protests.

There proved to be, not only one kitten, but three.

We named them, Pearl, Diamond, and Ruby.

Moonflower nursed them devotedly, Hadji lending a hand.

Lotus-Blossom was not allowed near the nursery. No matter how hard she tried, the mother refused to allow her access. Lotus Blossom developed a hacking cough which persisted. Zig continued her warring activities, preventing Lotus Blossom from taking up residence.

As the days passed, I realized Lotus Blossom was very ill, as she had grown so thin. I held her in my arms, sang to her, rocked her as I walked outside with her, put antibiotics down her throat, to no avail. She grew worse. The Vet called, a rare thing, for he usually saw the animals at his Surgery. He told me it was useless to try to save Lotus Blossom, but, seeing my distress, he gave her an injection. She cried piteously, so I brought her inside, cradled her in my arms. As ill as she was, she tried to sound her musical purring.

When she began to shiver, I placed a hot water-bottle under a towel, and put Lotus Blossom on her warm cushion. She died at 11 p.m. in our house.

We buried her under the trees in our garden, placed her name, the date of her demise, together with the words: 'Ave Maria – Love' on her Headstone.

When Moonflower allowed her kittens to leave their nursery, they tumbled about to their hearts' content.

My husband watched them through the kitchen window, amused at their antics. He called them, his 'toys'.

Hadji sat in the sun, observing the trio, with happy, proud look. Moonflower nestled against her Ginger-coloured hero, licking his fur with delicate tongue, rubbing against him, curling up within his embrace, when the kittens slept.

It was a joy to witness such deep devotion.

The weeks slipped by. I concocted bread cubes dipped in honey, and swimming in warm milk, at tea-time, for our cat-family outside. They loved it. Cream was also highly acceptable, as was jam-covered bread-cubes, soaked in milk.

Then, one day, disaster struck.

Ruby, the smallest kitten, came back from a 'survival' course, bleeding from one eye. Had she hurt it against barbed wire, or had a thorn pierced it? I could not pick Ruby up to examine her wounded eye, because Moonflower stood fierce guard over her children, spitting with rage as anyone drew near.

How deeply Moonflower had been scarred inside, if after two years with us, she still did not trust our species.

Worried, I could only hope that Ruby would heal.

The kittens were two months old, when their mother was killed by a car. My husband and I picked up the beautiful cat-lady, the very first time we had ever touched her. She had been struck on the head, but there were no injuries apparent, save for blood on her mouth, indicating there had been internal haemorrhage. After we had kept her body two days in the shed, we buried her beside Lotus Blossom. She too, received a Headstone, with the same words: 'Ave Maria – Love.'

And now, Ruby came towards me, crying. I picked her up. She was shivering. Bringing her inside, I placed her in the cat-basket, drove her to the Vet. He shook his head. I brought her home, amazed that the little bundle of fur rested so quietly against my heart with her eyes closed, purring quietly.

I carried her all day. That night, she slept on my bed. Something wakened me round 2 a.m. Switching on the light, I found that Ruby had fallen on to the carpet. Crying out, I rushed to pick her up, cradled her against my heart, weeping at my helplessness, at his distress.

My husband sat up. Tears came to his eyes.

Ruby died in my arms.

We lay her down beside her lovely mother.

Heart-sore, we watched Pearl and Diamond shadow their father. The latter was restless, searching everywhere for Moonflower, gazing, as did the kittens, at the road, at the fields, waiting, waiting, for that porcelain figure they loved – but, she never came. Hadji disappeared, never to return.

And now, fierce winds blew, causing us deep concern for the orphans who had been left entirely on their own. Two forlorn figures, still searching for their family.

Pearl was the male. He took charge. It was he, who led his sister to a place somewhat less buffeted by the wind. He sheltered Diamond with his body. They came for their meals as usual, but we grew more worried as winter drew ever nearer. I placed another box outside, hoping the pair would take shelter in it, as for some reason they refused to enter the old nursery…too many memories, perhaps.

Diamond crept into the box, her brother crouched over her shivering body, blanketing her from the bitter bite of the wind rushing in from the North.

I held a saucer of warm milk close to the box. The pink tongues drank thirstily.

Next, we drove to town, bought a clothes-basket in rattan, which I placed in the midst of our turf. Inside this basket were fluffy jerseys. To our joy, the pair came to investigate, cautiously entered, and remained there for thirty-six hours. They slept.

Snug as it was, the basket was not the place for them when winter's icy blast hit the land. They would not survive, I felt.

I decided to act! My husband and I cleared one room of its furniture. We put down linoleum on which we lay an old carpet, then, I took my cat-basket, and placed it near the clothes' basket. I waited. Diamond went in first, followed by Pearl, as usual, sheltering and protecting his sister. I had banked on that. With a pounce, I closed them inside the basket.

Triumphantly, I entered the house, having kidnapped the pair. Into the room they went. I closed the door. So far, so good.

I slept well that night. We had decided we would refurbish that room when Pearl and Diamond had become used to us, so we were not perturbed at claw-marks on the wallpaper.

Cardboard boxes, coloured balls of wool, pieces of bright ribbons, provided entertainment during the day. Diamond was terrified of being imprisoned, but her brother, whom we soon named 'the Sage', soothed her. He was very calm, staring at us with gratitude and love. His composure was a constant source of surprise to us. He appeared to know that we meant them well.

Soon, we allowed brother and sister to play about the living room. When I wanted them back in their playroom, I produced 'La Vache Qui Rit' cheese to them, enticing them back to their quarters on a happy note.

When two weeks had gone by, we allowed Pearl to go out on his own, whilst I carried Diamond outside in my arms. I spoke to her as we went along, aware that she made no move to get away from me.

Zig and Zag, were furious, staring at the intruders, with raised back and mouths which spat out cat-anger.

Pearl looked on, totally disinterested. Diamond cowered under the sofa.

When we thought it was time, we let Diamond go out as well. She gazed about her for awhile, looked at me, a trifle uncertain. I walked past her, uttering soothing words, she followed, unaware of my trepidation.

Would she return, or would she revert back to her wild, fearful self?

One must take chances in life.

A short while later, the lovely, sloe-eyes, so like her mother's, looked across the kitchen floor at me: 'Anything good to eat? Have you some cream, maybe?'

We were overjoyed.

Our wild cats were safe. Winter would not, please God, harm them.

Zig screamed at the 'enfants terrible' one day, from her perch high above them, telling them in no uncertain cat-terms, that she would definitely not put up with such boisterous behaviour. How dare they chase her, the Matriarch, up a tree!

Zag, alias John Wayne, the Marshal, spat and made a round back, whenever they drew near, manifesting his displeasure. As Pearl grew older, it was soon the Marshal's turn to avoid the powerful male, at all costs.

We refurbished our room, the four cats somehow made an uneasy truce at night when they had perforce to share the same living space, and peace settled for a time.

Diamond made it a habit of curling her body high up on my chest, whilst I watched Television at night. On my lap was Zig, determined no one would take away her human cushion.

Pearl settled in my husband's arms, content to fix his golden eyes on us all.

Zag arched his back, spat, came over to be caressed, then, lay down on the settee and went to sleep.

It was amusing to see how Diamond licked yoghurt from a spoon. She was very fond of desserts. Another of her unique features, was the way she reversed through the open window when coming in. Clever as she was, she quickly realized that she would fall off the narrow ledge outside, if she attempted to turn, so she improvised and came in, backwards. Her brother never thought of this trick, and we saw him plummeting to earth when we opened the window which swung outwards, but he was quickly up and inside, safe and sound. Zig was too dignified to use such methods, for her, it was the humans who had to play Door-person.

About a year later, a new neighbour moved in, bringing with her, about forty cats.

One of them was a black and white female, with only three legs. She had been attacked (so we were told), by dogs, and had thus lost a limb.

My husband and I saw her peeping at us from a bush. We ignored her, knowing she lived down the road. She had other plans.

With dogged persistence, she crept into the house, trying to insinuate herself into dark corners, but she gave herself away by growling every time she came near to us. My husband threw cushions at her, newspapers... he chased her out, closed the door. When it was opened again to admit our cats, she was in again.

This went on for weeks. One afternoon, I saw a small head peeping out from under the coat-rack, veiled by a long rain coat. Out, she went.

Next, she took up a position curled behind my Computer. I pretended not to see her. With a sigh of relief, she went to sleep in a graceful ball.

My husband and I wearied of chasing this cat-person away. She crept into the kitchen. Our cat-family menaced her. She confronted them all, a tiny paw raised threateningly, growls issuing from her throat: 'Just you try it,' she seemed to tell them, 'you will rue the day you ever tangled with me.'

They backed off.

When Pearl made a charge, she faced him bravely, diminutive paw lashing out at him. He never bothered her again, in fact, they became great playmates.

Eventually, we gave in with good grace.

The neighbour down the road had collected 'Hester' twice, to bring her back to her home, but each time, the black and white bombshell, came back. It was no use. She had decided that this was to be her home.

I told her mistress that we would adopt her. I changed her name to 'Black Magic', for her mystery, beauty, will-power, demanded another name – a more spectacular one.

She sat at times, watching Television, eyes avidly fixed on the screen, ears pricked, tail twitching. We put a box on the floor for her, having discovered her penchant for it as a television chair. After that, she exchanged the box for a golden-coloured cushion.

Black Magic was very affectionate, rushing to greet every cat-member with friendly nose-sniffing. By now, the others had accepted this dynamo of energy roving about them, like a mini-cyclone, entertaining everyone regularly with her Cabaret Show as she twirled about like a whirling Dervish, chasing her tail with breathtaking speed, grace and agility.

Our last defences had come tumbling down when we had put her out – again – one afternoon, only to glimpse a dog in the yard. We had opened the door to find Black Magic clinging to the outer mesh-door, which she had climbed to escape the canine. That was it! She had earned her right to a commitment on our part.

Tiny, dainty, delicately-formed, courageous, adventurous, affectionate, she was monarch of all she surveyed.

Zig, the matriarch, learned to accept with grace and with recently-acquired tolerance, the new arrivals. She remained as dignified as ever, totally in control. She was independent, disliked the brushing and combing I regularly subjected her to, had a partiality for chicken, and was a tigress in a fight, unlike Zag who was definitely a pacifist – a Marshal without hardware.

The latest addition to our cat-family was Tortoisehell, a male who was abandoned by his owners, no doubt because he had mange.

I had seen him on the property for some time, as he ate and drank outside. It was only when he came up to me for companionship, that I saw the large, ugly patches on his body. I recognized mange.

Knowing it had to be treated immediately, I picked him up, and dabbed the Benzyl Benzoate lotion on his wounds. He tried to wriggle free, but I held him fast.

'Be careful,' cautioned my husband, 'he may scratch you.'

That was a risk I was prepared to take. I had seen dreadful cases of mange, especially in Mauritius, and in African Townships.

Beautifully marked, with buff, ginger and black, Tortoiseshell looked at me with slanted eyes in which I detected a wistful longing. Of course I understood.

'I want to be loved!' is a universal cry.

Pearl chased Tortoiseshell. It was to be expected.

Tortoiseshell was as good as gold, allowing me to put Holy Water from Knock on his ugly wounds, as well as the lotion. Within a few weeks, the mange had disappeared. The newcomer dogged my footsteps, sprang on my lap, staring at me with love-laden eyes, paws kneading my jersey as he purred loudly.

At night I placed him in the spare bedroom, out of reach of Pearl's powerful resentment.

On day, Zag, the Marshal, failed to come home. We searched high and low for him, to no avail. One of our cat-family had left his physical shell. Perhaps he had been hit by a car, and had crawled into the thickets? Zag was no doubt with Prowler, and with all those wonderful souls who had graced my life for a time, in that Rainbow-Realm where suffering and strife is no more.

The Saga continued to unfold.

*   *   *

A VISION OF HOPE

Alick McInnes was a man who could feel the radiation from flowers. He explains: 'Everything radiates wavelengths which can be identified as sound, colour, form, movement, perfume, temperature and intelligence...everything created is interdependent. It follows that what affects one form of life must affect all other forms as well. If we deliberately cause suffering and disease in other lives we increase our own suffering and disease. All creation...is affected by disease inflicted on laboratory animals in what I believe to be a futile and foredoomed attempt to combat illness. All creation is tormented through the ghastly agonies which the vivisectionist inflicts on helpless creatures. Any relief of illness supposed to be removed by knowledge gained at the expense of such agonies will be paid for many times over in increased suffering in some other part of the whole. All creation suffers when plants in their millions are burnt by chemical weed-killers.

'Just as every created thing takes a knock for every victim of war or every inmate tortured in a concentration camp, so every created thing takes a knock when a rabbit dies of human-induced myxamatosis, when animals are hunted and killed for sport, or when terrified cattle are slaughtered in abattoirs. All of life is one. There is no exception!' 6

'Reverence for life', is a term Hindus translate as 'ahimsa' or harmlessness, where it is understood to mean that one should go through life, seeking to harm none in either thought, word, or deed.

This noble aspiration should be embraced by everyone.

In recent times S.Q. has suddenly appeared on the scene. Words such as 'spiritual awareness', 'spiritual workshops' are being used in the work-place, the home, even in the doctor's surgery.

It means 'Spiritual Quotient', that mysterious 'something' one must strive for, in order to achieve true happiness.

Suddenly, people are beginning to sit up and take notice of counsels handed down to us from the distant past, scattered like everlasting seeds in a universal language:

Chinese:	' What you do not wish done to yourself do not unto other.'
Hindu:	' The true rule is to guard and do by the things of others as they do by their own.'
Zoroastrian:	' Do as you would be done by.'
Buddhist:	'One should seek for others the happiness one desires for oneself.'
Muslim:	' Let none of you treat your brothers in a way he himself would dislike to be treated.'
Judaism:	' What ever you do not wish your neighbour to do to you, do not unto him.'
Christian:	' All things whatsoever ye would that men should do unto you, do ye even so unto them.'

In the Scriptures we are told that Wisdom stands at our Gates, crying out for our attention. The Spiritual Quotient emerging in our midst is focusing hearts and minds on the Inner, suggesting that worldly veils are being discarded, because mankind longs for the spiritual space Odyssey, and yearns to claim its true birthright!

The animal kingdom, insects, plants, minerals, also have their S.Q. They cannot be excluded from the Sacredness which unites us all in the Divine 'I AM'.

'Spiritual awareness 'will banish vivisection and animal experiments in laboratories. Abattoirs as they exist to-day, will be seen to be barbarous places; blood sports will cease to have their champions – everywhere, people will demand these changes, for Truth is not exclusive, it breathes the very spirit of universal charity and sympathy, extending healing hands to all.

Once, this spirit of gentle pity reigned, when Buddha the Enlightened One, stood before King Bimbisara and his court. Sir Edwin Arnold, in his 'Light of Asia', describes how the Blessed One spoke up, for these helpless creatures, so tormented by man:

'Then some one told the King, "There cometh here
a holy hermit, bringing down the flock
Which thou didst bid to crown thy sacrifice."
The King stood in his hall of offering,
On either hand the white-robed Brahmans ranged
Muttered their mantras, feeding still the fire
Which roared upon the midmost altar. There
From scented woods flickered bright tongues of flame......
Round about the pile
A slow, thick, scarlet streamlet smoked and ran,
Sucked by the sand, but ever rolling down,
The blood of bleating victims. One such lay,
A spotted goat, long-horned, its head bound back
With munja grass; at its stretched throat the knife
Pressed by a priest...

But Buddha softly said,
"Let him not strike, great King!" and therewith
Loosed the victim's bonds, none staying him, so great
His presence was. Then, craving leave, he spake
Of life, which all can take but none can give,
Life which all creatures love and strive to keep,
Wonderful, dear, and pleasant unto each,
Even to the meanest; yea, a boon to all
Where pity is, for pity makes the world
Soft to the weak and noble for the strong.
Unto the dumb lips of his flock he lent
Sad pleading words, showing how man, who prays
For mercy to the god, is merciless.
Being as god to those; albeit all life
Is linked and kin, and what we slay have given
Meek tribute of the milk and wool, and set
False trust upon the hands which murder them…

Thus spake he, breathing words so piteous,
With such high lordliness of ruth and right,
The priest drew down their garments o'er the
Hands
Crimsoned with slaughter, and the King came near,
Standing with clasped palms reverencing Buddh;
And through the land next day passed a decree
Proclaimed by criers, and in this wise graved
On rock and column: "Thus the King's will is: -
There hath been slaughter for the sacrifice
And slaying for the meat, but henceforth none
Shall spill the blood of life nor taste of flesh.
Seeing that knowledge grows, and life is one,
An mercy cometh to the merciful."
So ran the edict, and from those days forth
Sweet peace hath spread between all living kind
Man and the beasts which serve him, and the birds…'

*   *   *

For peace to become a reality, society needs to become more and more aware of the imperative to outlaw cruelty.

I dare to have a vision where Abattoirs will no longer exist as they are today. We will have discovered a humane manner in which to obtain the meat society is intent on consuming. We have many brilliant minds among us. They will find a way to put the animals gently to sleep, then their hearts will be made to stop, so ensuring a painless, anguish-free death. I dare to dream that one day this will happen. Also, do I dare to contemplate the outlawing of vivisection, that most cruel practice.

Once, I was very ill, and my mother took me to Switzerland for a cure. She did not give me any clue as to what this cure entailed. I therefore went to the Clinic to which she brought me with such great motherly love, and submitted to the tests asked of me. The next day I was to receive the 'treatment.' That night I had a dream. I saw a piece of ground on which lay dead sheep, and blood was everywhere. Then, the scene vanished, and I saw the back of a man, standing with arms outstretched. From his hands came forth a golden light, and where the sheep had been lying, there was lovely white sand, pristine and lovely. I was struck forcefully by this dream, and told the doctor who was to treat me, about it. I then enquired what was this treatment he was about to give me. He had perforce to tell me. It was the introduction of 'live cells' into my body. The mother sheep had her baby killed within her womb and these cells were to be injected straight into my body. I was horrified to hear this, and decided to refuse the treatment forthwith, to my mother's great sorrow, for I was in fact very ill. She had to follow me out of the Clinic, and we boarded a bus. A woman sympathised with my mother as she sat weeping, and enquired what was the matter. My mother told her. The woman looked at me, then smiled: 'Do not cry, Madame. There is a healer close by. His name is Monsieur Pittet. The bus stop is near to his gate. I will take you to him.' True to her word, she led us to the healer's home, then she left us. Surely an angel sent to help us. When we entered the interior of this house, we were greeted by a charming old man who listened closely to my mother's tale, then he asked me to come forward and he began to examine my face. He took a pendulum out of a drawer and held it over my one hand.

'You love both East and West,' he said, then smiled at me. 'That is rare. What have the doctors done to you, my poor Madame.' He shook his head.

He went behind me and placed his hands on my shoulders. There was a warm feeling coming from them, and I began to feel soothed.

'Your shoulder has been dislocated,' he observed, 'I shall fix that now.'

I had in fact been suffering from that shoulder for months, and had been unable to serve at tennis, after my operation.

In no time he had fixed my shoulder. I was delighted.

Next, he told my mother some facts about my health when I was an infant in Madagascar where I was born. My mother was amazed. Every detail was true.

Monsieur Pittet gave me herbs to take, and bade us good cheer. He refused payment of any kind.

That night, for the first time in months, I slept. Also, I was able to eat with appetite. From that day on my health improved until I was my old self again. I corresponded with Monsieur Pittet, grateful to him for his great kindness to me.

This experience taught me that there is a wonderful Power at work in our lives, and if we are true to our heart's impulses and principles, then, we have no need to fear anything.

What had caused me to have that dream warning me that animals were to die in order for me to have that treatment?

What strange coincidence had caused us to meet that lady on the bus?

Who can deny these marvellous happenings?

I have been humbled and awed so many times by such interventions in my life.

And so, I trust my dreams, seeing them as emerging from a Wise Somewhere, and, above all, I trust in the Divine Love Which shapes all our ends.

One day, Society will reject the Abattoirs as they exist this day. Society will do away with animal experiments. We are told they are essential for the good of our health. If I am to continue my life on this earth by causing untold agony in laboratories, then I refuse. As simple as that. I reason thus. I know death is a certainty. Why shall I cling to this life through the agony of animals.....? No. Always, No.

And so, yes, I dare to see a humane Society emerge one day. When the younger generation realize that the Whole is One, they will perhaps insist on these changes. Animals, insects, are all the jewels in the Diadem of God. Let us never lose sight of this. If this is Utopic, then let it be so. I cannot, and will not, give up on the human capacity for compassion and mercy. It may take time, But one day it will appear – just as flowers appear eventually.......even the very slow growers!

Lord Halden stated; 'The Way to the truth lies in idealism. The finite and the infinite appear in the end to be no longer independent existences. The higher comes out as the most real, and it is always the more spiritual that appears as the highest. The belief that the more experience is spiritual the more it is real has influenced me through the course of life...'

The scientist, Fritjof Capra writes: 'The basic oneness of the universe is not only the central characteristic of the mystical experience but is also one of the most important revelations of modern physics...the unity of all things and events will be a recurring theme throughout our comparison of modern physics and Eastern philosophy...Quantum theory thus reveals an essential interconnectedness of the universe. It shows that we cannot decompose the world into independently existing smallest units...Quantum theory forces us to see the universe not as a collection of physical objects, but rather as a complicated web of relations between the various parts of a unified whole...the picture of the interconnected cosmic web which emerges from modern atomic physics has been used extensively in the East to convey the mystical experience of nature...in Eastern mysticism, this universal interwoveness always includes the human observer and his or her consciousness, and this is also true in atomic physics...mystical knowledge can never be obtained just by observation, but by full participation with one's whole being.' 7

Herbert Spencer mused on the Infinite and Eternal Energy, thus; 'But one truth must grow ever clearer – the truth that there is an Inscrutable Existence everywhere manifested, to which we can neither find nor conceive beginning or end. Amid the mysteries which become the more mysterious the more they are thought about, there will remain the one absolute certainty that we are ever in the presence of an Infinite and Eternal Energy from which all things proceed.'

It is comforting to know that we are not, as we sometimes imagine, tiny life-specks, buffeted about by an indifferent Fate, in an alien, hostile world, only to taste annihilation at the end of our life-cycles. We are related to the Whole. There are no 'dead' particles in the Universe. Everything pulsates with energy, with life. Forms simply undergo transmutation.

We must radically transform our busy, work-a-day lives, by infusing them once again with the Sacred Presence as in days long gone, in order to set free in us the creative intuition which permits us to see beneath the surface of things, to delight in the contact with the fascinating abundance which is the fullness of our universe; we touch, as it were, the supernatural potential which cannot be diminished because it proceeds from eternal being. We break through our own limited sphere, ego-restricted, penetrating the hidden depths of our being, realizing timeless truths.

We build from within, and we attract from without.

Everything is first worked out in the unseen, before it is manifest in the seen, a divine sequence which runs through the entire universe.

The false values of avarice and ignoble ambition, must be replaced by reason and love. We need to develop a heart of wisdom. This is brought about by inner discipline.

Every today, builds to-morrow, as this Sanskrit proverb tells us:

'Look to this day, for it is life
The very life of life.
In its brief course lies all
The realities and verities of existence.
The bliss of growth, the splendour of action
The glory of power.
For yesterday is but a dream,
And tomorrow a vision of hope.
Look well, therefore, to this day.'

Saintly, Mother Teresa of Calcutta, said it was the duty of every individual to be holy.

It is high time humanity travels along the Highway of Hope, beholding skies aflame with starlight. Above all, we must learn to forgive.

There is a magnificent poem by Robert Buchanan, which illustrates Divine forgiveness. I give the last verses here:

'Twas the soul of Judas Iscariot
Stood black, and sad and bare;
I have wandered many nights and days;
There is no light elsewhere.
'Twas the wedding guests cried out within,
And their eyes were fierce and bright:
Scourge the soul of Judas Iscariot
Away into the night!
The Bridegroom stood in the open door,
And he waved his hands still and slow,
And the third time that he waved his hands
The air was thick with snow.
And every flake of falling snow,
Before it touched the ground,
There came a dove, and a thousand doves
Made sweet sound.

'Twas the body of Judas Iscariot
Floated away full fleet,
And the wings of the doves that bare it off
Were like its winding sheet.
'Twas the Bridegroom stood at the open door,
And beckoned, smiling sweet;
'Twas the soul of Judas Iscariot
Stole in and fell at his feet.
The Holy Supper is spread within
And the many candles shine
And I have waited long for thee
Before I poured the wine.
The supper wine is poured at last,
The lights burn bright and fair
Iscariot washes the Bridegroom's feet,
And dries them with his hair.'

*　　　*　　　*

Sometimes, walking in the Autumn across the fields, I have chanced upon a tiny flower-face peeping at me from withered grasses, a star springing from Mother's Bosom, like a brooch of light! At such a sight, my heart bows in wonder: 'Brave one, it is so cold, and yet you shine! Little warrior, I salute you!'

Our cat people left us one by one.

Diamond died near the house, and her lovely form was placed beside that of Ruby and Moonflower. Next, Black Magic contracted cancerous growths, and she looked at me with her lovely eyes as the Vet stopped her pain and her life. With a Rosary about her neck, she was buried with flowers all about her, in our Animal Sanctuary.

Then, it was Zig who was became terminally ill, and once again I held a velvety paw as she was put to sleep. Under the beautiful trees she was placed, also a Rosary around her neck.

Pearl was in great pain. Our friend, the Vet, ended his anguish. Strong, brave, wise Pearl was with the other children who had left us – dancing in the Sky Realm.

Tortoiseshell was the only survivor.

And then the dark wings touched my beloved husband. He lay dying at home, and Tortoiseshell gently settled near Vincent's legs, curling up to comfort and give love. My husband's pale hand tenderly reached to stroke him. And then, my husband left this Realm for a Greater MORE.

Tortoiseshell came to me, love streaming from his eyes. He was my shadow, loving and faithful.

At night, Tortoiseshell settled close to me, his paw on my lap, his eyes gazing into mine. He seemed to be saying: 'I am here. I love you. We will get by, you and I. Have no fear.'

Seven months later, I saw Tortoiseshell crawl into the house, one leg dragging behind him. Uttering a cry I scooped him up into my arms, and I realized he was very badly hurt. Placing him on a cushion, I phoned my Vet, but he was away, and I had to wait several hours before I could see another. My worst fears were realized. Tortoiseshell had been run over by a car and his leg was broken in several places......... I was told I would have to go to Galway, to the Veterinary Clinic there. However, it being the week-end, I would have to wait two days.

I was frantic with worry. What to do? I was given pain-killers to administer to Tortoiseshell, and with trepidation I took him to Galway. The Vet was very gentle. My Tortoiseshell was taken away for X-Rays. Then, he underwent an operation. When I went to collect him, Tortoiseshell had his leg and hip in a type of 'cage'. Every week the Vet would have to move the pins. What an ordeal for my cat-child! And so, throughout the winter months of that year,

Tortoiseshell and I endured. He the discomfort and pain, and I, watching his ordeal.

Tortoiseshell was very brave – stoical. It must have hurt him to have those pins moved every week, yet he never held it against me. Wise as ever, he came to me to be comforted and to comfort in turn. My heart ached to see him in that 'cage', and I did all I could to make him comfortable. He had a box by the fire so that he could enjoy the heat, but his eyes were fixed on me, love shining in their depths.

The months went by, and then the great day. I brought Tortoiseshell home triumphant, his legs free of the constricting 'cage'. What joy in his eyes – and in mine!

I watched him walk about enjoying his freedom, although I had to be cautious, as the Vet had warned me that it would still be some weeks before Tortoiseshell would be out of danger, because of the possibility of shattering the bones which had just knit. I therefore took him outside on a lead, until the bones were strong enough. The Vet had explained that sometimes when an animal has had such severe breakage in the bones, a sudden leap could harm the bones and shatter them. However, the perilous time passed and then Tortoiseshell took off on his own again.

There was a certain caution however, as he did not stay away long. I watched him with joy. He could have been killed by the speeding car, as had another cat along the road from where I lived. The Vet had performed a brilliant operation, and I was grateful.

For a few months all was well, then I noticed that Tortoiseshell began to bring up his food on a regular basis. My visits to the Vet became more frequent, until one day my friend looked at me and told me very gently that Tortoiseshell was dying……his kidneys had been very badly hurt in the accident. With his lovely golden eyes looking into mine, Tortoiseshell was put to sleep.

My friends came for his funeral. A Rosary about his neck, a picture of Padre Pio, flowers….

He was laid beneath the whispering trees in our Animal Sanctuary. A Chinese Kite was sent up into the Sky to celebrate Tortoiseshell's entry into Heaven. My beloved, loyal, brave Tortoiseshell was the last of my children to leave me.

And now, I live here in my home, my spirit on the Rainbow within, and there, we are all together. There, within the Heart-Realm, there is love, joy, happiness and no parting.

When people ask me how I can dwell in such solitude I tell them I am never alone.

First of all, there is my Guardian Angel who is ever at my side, then, all those who have blessed me with their love.....no, I am not alone.

My Odyssey continues. Life is a marvellous adventure. One must fear nothing.

As the great Sage, Sri Bhagavan Ramana Maharshi once said: 'If you board a train, you do not hold on to your luggage, but place it on a rack and seat yourself. So too, must you relax and allow the Train of Life to carry you on your journey.'

This lesson is such a great one. To allow the One Whose Power created you, to bear you along the destiny which is your own. To relax is vital, for trust in God confers serenity such as one cannot imagine, but can only experience.

And so, we must be brave on this Odyssey of ours. We must not falter. Stumble we do, yes, often, but always, we must go on.

Love everything. It is the key of life.

Intuitive perceptions of truth will become our daily bread, as we unfold spiritually.

We must hold in our hearts a radiant Vision for Society, which we have a right to vizualize. A future where cruelty will be anathema; where pain will be a thing of the past when undergoing the 'dying' process; when old, frail beings will be cared for, with the gentleness and care, they richly deserve; when the helpless, the abandoned, the vulnerable (of all species), will fall into 'tender' hands.

I recall how I once heard cries of desperation coming from a hospital room one night. Going to investigate, I found a young man thrashing about on his bed, in anguish. As I leaned over him, his eyes met mine: 'Stay with me,' he entreated, 'don't leave me alone.'

'Are you in pain?' I had asked, deeply concerned.

'No. I just cannot bear to be so alone.'

Loneliness is indeed a terrible pain. In this bright future I dare to see, are included hospitals having voluntary workers in this field, holding the hands of the sick, listening to the stories pouring from overburdened hearts, or, simply just being a silent presence, comforting them.

In another hospital, once an old lady beckoned me to her side: 'I like your face,' was her surprising comment, 'so, I will tell you a secret. This old body of mine, lies here, waiting for its end, but I am in truth flying, dancing. I have nothing to do with this body of mine.' Her eyes shone with joie-de-vivre: 'I have lived my life to the full, tasted joy, tasted sorrow, and I have no regrets.

One must never have regrets, you know. Who would be silly enough to drink vinegar? I lie here, looking about me, watching people come and go. They cast their eyes on me, and no doubt, think to themselves: 'Poor, old creature…won't be long now.' She pulled such a comical face, that we both laughed. She went on: 'Then, you smiled at me from across the room, and I thought:" She is nice. I will tell her my secret…that I am dancing inside…"'

Startled, struck with wonderment, I held this lady's hand as she launched into some tales about her long life.

That was a lesson I never forgot. Appearances are very deceptive.

Another time, when I was caring for some handicapped women, a nun who was in charge of elderly patients, came to ask me a favour. One man who was terminally ill, had waited until 9 p.m. the previous night, for his son's visit, only to suffer bitter disappointment when he did not appear. She finished with the words: 'He needs what I cannot give him, being a nun. He needs a kiss and a big hug.'

This nun was very dear to me. I went along with her to where a pale-faced man stared out of a window.

Sister told him: 'See, here is the French lady I told you about.'

In no time, an animated look came over his features. I gave the Gaelic hugs and kisses on both cheeks. He died that night.

That wise woman had realized how desperate is the heart, for love, warmth, tenderness. It is the very breath of life. We must never withhold it.

To thine own self be true. Integrity is a treasure we must never part with. It must never be sold for a mess of pottage.

The remarkable work of Doctor Clarissa Pinkola Estes, emphasises this integrity of spirit, one should always strive for. She writes: 'Perhaps most elementally, the Bluebeard story raises to consciousness the psychic key, the ability to ask any and all questions about oneself, about one's family, one's endeavours, and about life all around…she is free to wrest the powers which were once used against her to her own well-suited and excellent uses. That, is a wildish woman.'   8

When Heart-Wisdom perfumes our lives, we will be able to say, as Tennyson did: 'I dreamed that stone by stone I reared a sacred fane, a temple, neither pagoda, mosque, nor church, but loftier, simpler, always open-doored to every breath from heaven, and Truth and Peace and Love and Justice came and dwelt therein.'

Mercy, compassion, will lead us to the Summit.

In the Hadith (collection of Sayings from the Prophet Muhammad), there is a lovely story of how a prostitute once passed by a well. She saw a dog dying of thirst. Quickly, she allowed a piece of her robe to collect water, which she then placed in the animal's mouth. For this act, we are told, all her sins were forgiven her.

William Buhlman, author of 'The Secret of the Soul', writes: 'There are numerous reports of people having seen a "silver cord" attached to their pet. The very nature of this connection points to a highly evolved spiritual component that appears similar if not identical to a human silver cord. I had such an experience in 1983. During an out-of-the-body experience, I saw my beagle puppy, MacGregor, walking along beside me. He appeared completely natural and solid as he wagged his tail and looked up at me. His eyes were shining, and there was a thin filament, like a spider web, stretching from his body and reaching back toward the bedroom where his physical body was sleeping. This was not something I had expected to see when out of body, and it forever changed my perception of animals.

'What I have found amazing is the fact that the so-called lower life forms can communicate with surprising intelligence when they are out of body. There are many reports of animals providing companionship, advice, and assistance to out-of-body travelers.

This may explain why several ancient cultures, such as that of the Egyptians, had a deep reverence for cats – one far surpassing the status we accord mere house pets. One of the oldest and most mysterious monuments of all time is the Sphinx. The magnificent stone creation clearly portrays the body of a great and noble cat with the face of a man. Many believe that the Sphinx signified for the ancient Egyptians the inherent intelligence and advanced evolution of that animal. Not only do animals have souls; they are obviously evolving alongside us. And this appears to be true of all animals, not just domesticated pets. Many believe that animals possess consciousness and should be treated with more respect that they now receive. A growing number of people feel that we need to reappraise our beliefs concerning our relationship with the animal kingdom. To expand our vision of evolution, consciousness, and soul, we must look beyond our assumptions about other forms of life. All physical life-forms are vehicles for consciousness, used to experience the dense realms of matter. These outer vehicles of soul form an integral element in the evolution of consciousness…We must remember that the various forms of matter are essentially tools and expressions of soul. Without this divine inner spark of consciousness, biological forms could not be animated. Is it possible that the soul of the giant redwood may be learning patience and that the soaring bird may be learning the freedom of flight? How can any soul truly learn and express these qualities except from personal experience?

.Evidence suggests that some animals, such as dogs and cats, may be close to the spiritual sophistication and evolution required for them to have their first human incarnation. Many people today believe that the soul evolves through the use of increasingly more complex biological life-forms – a process generally perceived as a progression of consciousness. Let us open our minds to a much broader vision of evolution and our path to the soul.' 9

Doctor Axel Munthe, (already introduced to the reader), whose inspiring life-story,' 'The Story Of San Michele' touched millions of hearts when his autobiography appeared in print, tells, how countless birds were being netted and put to death, on a mountain belonging to a butcher. When the latter fell ill, he required the doctor's services. He was told that medical help would be forthcoming only if he sold this mountain to the Doctor. The butcher agreed, and, in this way, a Sanctuary was created for the birds.

The Doctor was one who understood that the central fact in human life, is the coming into a conscious, vital realization of our oneness with the Infinite Life.

Samuel Taylor Coleridge sums up Religion, in the superb words of the Ancient Mariner:

'He prayeth well who loveth well
Both man, and bird and beast.

He prayeth best who loveth best
All things both great and small;
For the dear God who loveth us,
He made and loveth all.'

*　　　*　　　*

Author's son with Snappy

Miko – Johannessburg

Sixpence my cat – Peacehaven office, JHB

Zig and Zig – Ireland

Author with Sita in Johannesburg

Author and Nou-Nou – Johannesburg

Rusty – Johannesburg

Li-Li – Johannesburg

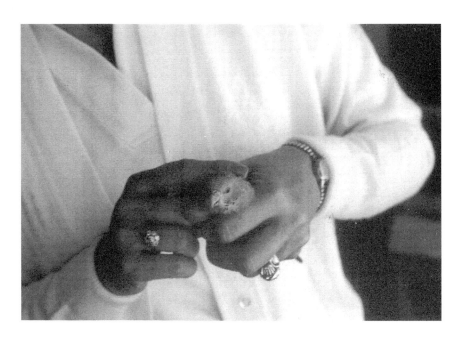

David Livingston – Johannesburg

Pearl – Ireland

Black Magic – Ireland

Tortoiseshell – Ireland

Cat Cemetery - Ireland

Zig - Ireland

NOTES

1   Peter Tomkins & Christopher Bird – The Secret Life of Plants – Penguin Books 1973

2   The Mountain Path – Aradhana Issue 1999 – Sri Ramanashramam – Tiruvannamalai South India

3   Paul Brunton – Hermit In The Himalayas – Rider & Co. London 1962

4   Arthur Osborne – The Mountain Path – Aradhana Issue 1999 – Sri Ramanashramam Tiruvannamalai – South India

5   Maurice Messegué –Health Secrets of Plants and Herbs – Allen & Unwin 1975

6   Peter Tomkins & Christopher Bird – The Secret Life of Plants – Penguin Books 1973

7   Fritjof Capra – The Tao of Physics – Fontana Collins 1976. Pp. 134. 141, 146

8   Clarissa Pinkola Estes, Ph.D.- Women Who Run With The Wolves – Ballantine Books New York 1992

9   William Buhlman – The Secret of the Soul –Harper Collins San Francisco 2001 pp.22, 23

*   *   *